KEYS TO KINDNESS

with Kindness

Dem

KEYS TO KINDNESS
My True Stories

Denelle Harris

ISBN: 978-1-0797-8093-2

Book design by Longworth Creative LLC

First Edition
Printed in the United States of America

To my Aunt Jean who showed me I had more stories to tell than I would ever have guessed.

CONTENTS

SPIRITUALITY

PERSONAL GROWTH

WORK/CAREER

ACKNOWLEDGEMENTS

I give my heartfelt gratitude for the encouragement and kindness of those who kept me writing. Janet Ross, who said I would write a book when I'd never considered doing such a thing, Bill Stevenson, who made me believe the stories were important, my sister, Jan Schirmeister, who listened and helped me tell these stories with truth and clarity, Sandi Howlett, who told me I am a powerful storyteller and "rememberer" with limitless compassion, Judy Bouise, who urged me to use my life as a way to encourage others to examine their own, Kathleen Osta who shared her "feel for flow", Vaughn Delp-Smith and Colette Ward, who gave me their writer's perspective.

I am deeply thankful to all those who urged me to write these stories down when they heard them over a period of thirty years. Especially Elaine Jordan, a masterful editor, who encouraged and convinced me I was a writer with worthwhile narratives to share, as well as Jennifer Longworth who helped me turn these stories into a meaningful book.

I would like to pay tribute to those of you who have listened; nurtured and mirrored back to me a gift I hope helps others: Scott Gilmore, Mary Ann Miller-Novak, Susan Crutcher, Bill Villani, Jerry Brown, Sherry Sheldon, Barbara Burnett, Lynn Lasry, and Bob Dittberner.

Above all I wish to humbly acknowledge my mother, Marcia Manigold, who taught me unconditional love and the importance of a sense of humor, my father Dean Manigold, who gave me motivation to succeed, my grandmother, Alice Mellon, and grandfather, Peter Manigold, who shared their life's wisdom.

I wish to express my love for my children, Alicia Hutchinson, Andy Tompkins, Adam Tompkins and grandchildren Chance, Shianne, Nick and Josh who give me the love, joy and strength to keep going in this life.

Be kind whenever possible.
It is always possible.

— The Dalai Lama

CE

f stories because
rstanding I've dis-
m. Knowing how
o changed my life.
hese experiences,
ple.

er the times I was
lt situations and
there to help me,
I also remember
beautiful healthy
e of raising them
long climb in my
many situations
ne stronger. I am
ities presented
hallenging or

As far back as I can remember, curiosity about people and their lives has been a part of me which couldn't be suppressed. Knowing the right questions to ask seems to be a gift I've been given—and the stories follow. The wisdom I gained, which I call Keys to Kindness, gave me insights, helped solve problems and bring new discoveries. I feel blessed when people say they've never told anyone else what they share with me. That happens all the time, whether in the grocery line or in the college class I've been facilitating for eleven years called 'The Wise Women Gathering'.

Many times over the years I've been told I should put these stories in a book. I didn't know how to write a book, so I put notes on sticky note pads as I told and heard them. Soon there were over a hundred. And I keep collecting more. There seems to be an endless supply of people's experiences worth being heard. I have been honored to witness the miracle of healing and awakening that comes from sharing our stories.

Maybe these episodes will inspire you to write down your own. My belief is that we all have narratives to share. Even children have their tales, and they feel special when someone takes the time to listen. At that moment, the storyteller and the listener share kindness and caring which can nurture and enlighten us.

CHILDREN, GRANDCHILDREN AND PARENTING

SOCKS

1974

For a time my seven-year-old son came home from school almost every day crying because there was a bully in his class who was threatening him. Luckily, I was a full-time mom who could be there when he got home. Today he was teary. I stopped folding the laundry. It was time to listen. I wanted to pay attention to this troubled little boy.

"I try to be nice," Adam said, looking like a miserable defeated little kid, "but he says he's going to beat me up anyway."

I set aside the stack of t-shirts. "Have you talked with Miss Morgan about it?"

"I tell her every day!" Tears coursed down his sad face. "Michael catches me on the playground when she isn't looking!"

I could feel myself getting angry about what was happening to this sweet soul. I wanted to tell Adam to pick up a rock, but curbed my mean thought. I took him over to sit in our rocking chair and pulled him onto my lap.

We rocked quietly. "I know it must hurt, honey. You'll think of a way to make Michael like you." I believed that if Adam were left to his own devices for just a little longer, he would come up with his own solution so I resisted giving him my ideas.

A few days later, Adam came home from school with a big smile on his face and said, "I fixed that guy." He took off his jacket and planted himself on a kitchen chair.

I got some Oreos out of the cupboard, poured us each a glass of milk, and sat with him to hear his story. "What did you do?"

"I told him if he didn't stop trying to scare me, I would eat my socks." He took a bite out of his cookie.

I laughed with delight. "What happened then?"

"That meany had this shocked look on his face...can I have some more milk?"

As I went to the refrigerator for the milk I said, "Good for you!" I thought of how I handled some of the unpleasant times with my unkind sister-in-law and wished I could be as brave as my son.

I look back now on that conversation and wonder where Adam got such a clever idea. After that, Michael became Adam's protector and bodyguard on the playground. They were good friends the rest of the year.

Given the opportunity kids can often be remarkably resourceful on their own.

NIGHT TIME MAGIC

1982

My sister, Jan, tells the story of one of her kids often waking in the night terrified of the monster in the bedroom. Of course, there wasn't a "monster," but it was real to that frightened little guy. He would be crying when he called to her.

She would come to his room and say, "Just a minute, I'll get the monster spray."

Off she would go to the bathroom where she had some watered down cologne in a spray bottle with just a hint of fragrance in it. She'd come back in the bedroom and spray around the room and under the bed.

Then she'd say, "There, no monsters will come in here now."

The little boy would snuggle under the covers, mom would kiss him soundly, tuck him in and he'd be off to dreamland before she got back to bed.

🔑 **Imagination is powerful "play" especially when it takes the fears away.**

RED FELT HAT

1975

Lane was one of my son Adam's best friends when they were both eight years old. The boys lived only three houses apart and were either at our house or Lane's almost every day. We lived on a quiet street in Phoenix, and the boys had similar interests — like board games they could enjoy indoors on hot summer days. They played outside at the park nearby when it was cooler.

Lane hadn't been in school for a few days, so Adam stopped by his house to see what the matter was. He was told that his buddy would be out of school for a while. Lane had leukemia.

He left Lane's house and came into the kitchen very upset and asked me, "What's leukemia? How did he get it? Is he going to die? Why didn't anyone tell me before?"

I was so shocked by the news that I stumbled over my words, trying to tell the truth and still be optimistic. I finally ended my explanation with, "You can visit Lane when his mom says it is okay. Leukemia isn't catching, and he must be pretty lonesome."

So they were together frequently. Adam would tell Lane what was happening at school, and they'd play together until suppertime. Lane's mother told me it was helpful for Adam to be there. It lifted Lane's spirits and helped her cope, too.

Soon the chemotherapy made Lane bald, and he was very self-conscious. My son had a solution. One day he came home from one of his visits and said, "I'm going to give Lane my red hat. He needs it." Now this hat was Adam's very favorite hat. He picked it out at the fair when he was just two years old. It was red felt and had his name written on the front of it. Because he had worn it a lot, it was tired and soft.

"That sounds like a great idea," I said, impressed by my son's thoughtfulness.

Adam gave his hat to Lane, and his mother told me the only way Lane would go out of the house was if he was wearing it.

In a year Lane was back in school, completely recovered. I like to think that Adam helped him get well, and I wonder if Lane still has that hat.

Loving kindness comes at all ages.

THERE ARE ONLY TWO RULES

1977

The first rule is: *You get what you give*, which is commonly known. The second rule: *You get what you think*, is not so easily understood. An example of the second rule is: the thought or idea of a table before it is made. A second example would be: You imagine the perfect partner and they show up in your life. I raised my kids with those beliefs. They understood them at a very early age. My youngest son, Andy, at four years old, understood them well and surprised me in a way I might not have expected.

One summer morning he came running into the house, a little breathless, wearing a blue t-shirt and red shorts, his blonde hair messed up and big blue eyes opened wide. He told me that our neighbor, Eunice, was going to be at our house any minute to tell me that he had hurt her son, Jimmy. I asked him what had happened. He said, "Jimmy hit me first, so I just did what you taught me. I gave him what I got. Only I did it harder and knocked him on the ground!"

When Eunice and Jimmy arrived at our house, I had to smile as I explained to them the principle that had led Andy to fight back. Everyone seemed to understand. Jimmy learned that Andy would always follow that rule and didn't start a fight with him again.

I also taught my kids: If you cause the trouble, you can expect to get into trouble. And the positive: If you are kind, you can expect kindness to be given to you in return.

Hopefully teaching these principles produces more fully functioning and loving human beings.

A CHILD'S UNDERSTANDING
1976

I was relaxing with my mother and a neighbor at my mother's pool in the Arizona shade that afternoon. Suddenly the neighbor's child came running through the gate shouting that John, my son's best friend, had drowned in the Salt River.

After a minute to take in the terrible news, we decided that I needed to go to John's mother right away. I raced home, got my purse and keys, got in the car and went to Carol. I found her pacing in the kitchen by herself.

"I got to him right away," she said, her eyes moving frantically, "but the branches were so tangled. I could touch the top of his head but couldn't get him out!" She was weeping, but couldn't stop telling her horrific story.

She and her neighbor had taken their kids to the river to float on their big inner tubes and have a picnic. "It was a beautiful day", she said, "and the tubes were tied together well. The kids all had safety vests on. Suddenly John's tube came untied and floated toward the overhanging branches that caught him. The river flow dragged him under. He was trapped."

John, at nine, was their oldest child, their only son.

I spent the rest of the day with Carol and her husband helping them get things organized with the funeral home, helping with notifications, standing by for whatever needed to be done, and witnessing their shock and sorrow.

It was ten o'clock when I got home that evening. My son, Adam, also nine years old, was waiting up for me. He knew that something bad had happened to John.

"He wouldn't go to sleep until you came home," my husband said. "He's in his bedroom."

When I got to his room I found him sitting on the edge of his twin bed, seeming very calm. He said, "I want to know exactly what happened. Tell me everything."

I hesitated a moment, wondering if he could take the truth. Then I sat next to him and decided to tell him what Carol had told me. He listened intently, not interrupting.

When I finished, Adam said, "It's like Halloween, Mom. John has just put on another costume. Now, whenever anyone thinks of him, he will be in their heart."

It gave me goosebumps. I wasn't sure how to respond. What a beautiful way to think of death, I thought. I held him close, so grateful that he was our son and still with us.

Ancient wisdom can live in the heart of a child.

AN INHERITANCE
1978

The future looked like a black hole. How could I possibly keep things together for my kids after a divorce? I was drowning in worry. Feelings of hopelessness and total incompetence clattered in my head. The voice of a former counselor, Jane, came to me. I decided to turn to her again and visited her charming office at the end of that week. I sat in a comfortable chair facing her.

After telling Jane my situation, she handed me paper and pen and said; "Make a list of your priorities."

I wrote *God, kids, extended family* and *home.* I recited my answers, and she told me to take more time and see if I could come up with more. I tried, but nothing came to me.

"Who sets the mood in the house?" she asked.

A strange question, but I thought about it and said, "I guess I do."

Jane looked at me for a minute. "If that's true, how come you're not first on the list?"

I had not thought of myself as a priority—before the children or my home, my friends and family? What a concept! What did she mean? That's not how I was raised. I was taught taking care of others first defined the "good woman". Otherwise I would be selfish. That idea was now turned upside down. If my happiness was creating the mood in the house, then I could see how important it was to put more focus on my wellbeing.

We talked about how my way of keeping our family life on an even keel had me at the bottom of the list. Jane convinced me that I needed to step back and see how I could find time for myself. She said, "Your children will be as okay as you ar

Now that I was a single mom I needed this counsel more than ever. She recommended some books about caring for the self as the best way to care for others. Reading them gave me a new perspective.

After eight months, the shock of facing divorce began to wear off. I was beginning to see some light in my life. I followed Jane's revelation and with the help of additional counseling, I felt stronger and more confident.

The kids were reassured that we would stay in our home, and we'd be able to go ahead with our lives. My ex-husband and I made agreements, a pact that we each would not criticize the other parent in front of the children and we would not allow the children to criticize us either. We kept our agreements, and my ex-husband, his wife and I now spend holidays together with the whole family in a joyful atmosphere.

The ultimate inheritance occurs when parents have a good sense of their own well-being that they can pass on to their children.

WISE OR UNWISE

1979

An Arizona summer day, about 115 degrees, and I'm driving home from work after another exhausting day. As I drive, I think about getting home to see the kids, the center of my life. Thinking about fixing something cool for dinner, I decide to make a taco salad and corn chips along with ice cold watermelon. The kids all love that. Finally home, I turn into the driveway, get out of the car and open the front door. The smell of something like burned matches hits my nose.

Adam, age twelve, Alicia, age nine, and Andy, age seven, are all there and the house is neatly picked up, kind of unusual.

Everyone greets me with a smile, "Hi, Mom," and a hug from my daughter. Her brothers are watching TV. I say, "Hello and what's that smell in the house?" At first no one says anything, and then I remind them, "You need to tell me the truth. You don't get into trouble if you tell the truth, remember? Adam, would you please turn off the TV, so we can talk about this?" The boys sprawl on the floor at my feet and Alicia sits on the couch with me.

Finally Alicia says, "Well, Terry came over to the house and showed us a new trick." Terry is a neighbor girl who quite often is the one who likes to make up untrue stories and get her and whoever else is around, in trouble. She is in junior high with my oldest son Adam.

I ask, "There isn't supposed to be anyone in the house besides the three of you when I'm working, right?" They look down with guilty expressions on their faces and say, "Yes, mom." I say, "Okay, that's one problem. Now what caused the burning smell?"

My youngest son, Andy, gets excited and says, "Terry showed us how to pour alcohol on our hands and light it. It was so cool and it doesn't even hurt!"

I follow that up with the question, "Do you think it was a wise decision for Terry to put alcohol on her hands and light it?"

They replied, "No!" in unison.

They seemed eager to confess and tell the whole story. Adam says that he made her stop doing it after a couple of times. I ask, "Do you think it was wise to stop her?"

Alicia says "Well, letting that go on could have hurt someone or burned down the house." The boys agreed with her. I complimented them on their wise thinking.

In my Women's Studies class at night school, our instructor, Joyce, suggested, "Teach your children to look at choices as wise or unwise, rather than good or bad." That seemed to be working in this situation. What I noticed was that the kids did not avoid the conversation, feel defensive or lie. Wouldn't most children like to be considered "wise"?

Using the terms "wise" or "unwise" allows the opportunity to consider all of the options without feeling judged as a "good" or "bad" person.

BRINGING UP ANDY

1979

I could see my twelve-year-old son in the mirror standing behind me, his blonde curls around his face. He said, "How come I can't live with you anymore?"

I turned around, took him by the shoulders and sat him down. Andy was the youngest and the hardest to raise. Though he was very bright, he was always in mischief, disruptive in school, and would not come home when he was supposed to. His behavior made home life chaotic for all four of us. At that time there was no diagnosis or treatment for ADD or ADHD, which we discovered years later, was part of the issue. As a working mom I couldn't ground him when he did something wrong, because I wasn't there to enforce it. I was so afraid he'd get into more serious trouble. It seemed my only solution was to send him to live with his dad across town.

"I just can't do this anymore," I told his father tearfully, and he agreed to take our son.

Andy looked sad as I explained that he'd been warned for over a year that he needed to behave better. I told him, "You were taught that you get what you give. I've been giving and you've been taking without any willingness to help or give back the love you've been getting."

He sat on my bed quietly listening. Maybe I'd gotten through.

I hugged him and told him, "I love you very much. This is the best thing for now." I cried so hard after he left.

Three years later, Andy was still having problems, so his dad and I took him to a therapist. I was sure I'd be blamed for sending him to live with his dad. But not a word was said about my parenting at our first family session. On our way out I asked the therapist, "When will Andy's issues with me come up? Nothing was said about that."

He said, "He has no issues with you. He knows you love him and always tell him the truth, even when he doesn't want to hear it.

I was astounded. For these three years I'd been feeling guilty about my decision. What a relief to know he understood what I had said and how much I cared for him.

He is now a successful business man and we are very close.

Telling a difficult truth with love to our children is one of the best gifts we can give them.

TREASURED
MOMENTS

1998

The nurse handed me a beautiful baby boy swaddled in his blanket just after his birth. His momma, my daughter, was still in the operating room, and his dad had asked me if I would take the baby while he stayed with her.

I looked at the infant in my arms. Here was my first grandchild! It gave me so much joy to be allowed to hold him. The nurse showed me to a rocking chair outside the nursery where we sat and rocked slowly together.

I held the baby close and whispered in his ear, "Hello, *Toko* Baby, this is your Nana and you are loved. Welcome to this world."

Then I repeated my greeting several times. The baby's eyes were open and he seemed aware of me and my words. He was very calm. I savored the smell of his skin, the feel of his beautiful, soft little fingers. It was a moment to cherish always.

I'd been told about this sweet boy before he was born when talking with a friend about my daughter's pregnancy. She shared that she had an intuitive message for the baby. She said, "There is a word, *Toko*, which the baby needs to hear when he is born. The word will ground him on this earth plane." So, "*Toko* Baby" became the nickname I used. His parents named him Nickolas.

When Nick was a teenager, I asked him if I should change his nickname to "*Toko* Boy." He said he liked it the way it was and still does.

Nick has now joined the Air Force. When I hugged him goodbye, I whispered in his ear, "Remember your lucky word is "*Toko*".

He smiled and said, "I will." It was hard to see him go, and I love and am so proud of him.

I look back now and treasure the memory of the day of his birth. That I could be there to support his mom and dad and hold my first grandchild was more wonderful than I could have imagined.

We only get *first* once.

AND THEN THERE WERE THREE

2000

It was a sunny summer day out in the countryside and I was walking down a dirt road with grass in the middle. On my hip, I was holding this darling dark-haired little girl who seemed about two and a half years old. She wore a denim blue sun dress with strawberries on it.

Walking by my side, holding my hand, was a slim four-year-old boy with light brown hair, wearing jeans and a yellow t-shirt. It was warm and we were all wearing sandals. I didn't know the children.

We walked toward a farmhouse hoping we could get a drink and make a phone call.

When we got near the door of the house, I woke up from the dream. It was so vivid, and I wondered what it all meant. I didn't think any more about the dream until two nights later when I dreamed it again.

When I woke—pondering what this could be concerning—the only thing that came to mind was that my oldest son, Adam, 28, and his wife, Jill, 35, had decided to adopt an older child, hoping they could help a child who had a difficult time being adopted. They had been trying for more than a year. Adam had told me that Jill was getting discouraged and close to wanting to quit. Adam persuaded her to try a little longer. I thought, "Maybe the dream was something related to that. Maybe I should say something to them. But what if I give them false hopes?" I didn't call.

Amazingly, four nights later I had the dream for the third time! "Okay," I thought, "I have to make that phone call and tell Adam." I called and told him, "I'm not trying to influence your thinking with false hopes, but I've had these three identical dreams in the last six days in which I am walking with these two small young children." I gave him the details of the story. He said, "It's okay, mom. Thanks for telling me. Don't worry about it causing us a problem."

Within four weeks I got a call from Adam telling me he and Jill had been introduced to a young dark-haired girl, age two and a half. Her name was Shianne, and they were starting adoption procedures. Shianne had a half-brother. He was four years old, slim, and had light brown hair. His name was Chance. The sad part was that the agency was trying to adopt them into different families even though they had been living in a foster care home for two years and were very close. Jill and Adam decided to adopt them both.

I became the grateful Nana to two wonderful grandchildren who were rescued from dire circumstances by two loving parents who gave them a new life.

Generous hearts can produce miracles in people's lives.

PRECIOUS TIMES
2001

My daughter, Alicia, was nearing the end of her second pregnancy. I was living in Oregon and she was in Arizona. We were trying to figure out what would be the best time for me to be there for the birth. We decided to plan for two weeks before the predicted due date.

As with many things, the plan changed. Alicia called me from the hospital saying Baby Josh was just born. So, I changed my flight to the following day. When I arrived at the hospital, I got to hold that sweet boy.

I was able to spend two weeks at Alicia's home, getting up with him for feeding and changing at night. Those were treasured times, just Josh and me. There's nothing like cuddling with a sweet new baby. When he was fed and changed, we would sit in the rocking chair in the living room and I would whisper to him about how beautiful and special he was.

It was also wonderful, caring for my daughter so she could rest. I made homemade meals to help her recover. The whole family especially liked their favorite fried chicken with mashed potatoes and gravy. I also got to play with and entertain Josh's brother, Nick, now three years old.

I cherished every moment, knowing in two weeks I would be leaving. The time flew by and it was my last night to get up with little Josh. We sat in the rocking chair, as always, and I told him how sad I was to be leaving, but that soon he would be able to come and visit me in beautiful Oregon. I promised to take him and his brother to the ocean beach which they had never seen.

We would build a sand castle and look for sea shells. He would get to play with our golden retriever, Ben, and that Ben would be so happy to have two cute little boys to play with.

I told him I loved him and promised that whenever he needed anything, I would help him as much as I could.

In 2010, my daughter and I both moved to Prescott where Josh had to start at a new school. I was fortunate enough to live nearby. When he didn't feel good enough to go to school, he would come over to stay with me. I'd tuck him in on the couch with the blanket with a soft satin edge. Then make his favorite scrambled eggs with toast and jelly and serve them to him in the living room so he could watch TV while he ate. Or I gave him rides to and from school when his mom was working. Later when he was a teen, I'd take him to get a favorite sandwich and one of those huge chocolate chip cookies after school when he was so hungry—like all teens are. As his Nana, those were precious times with him.

Sometimes I'd give him money he needed and he'd say, "You don't have to do that, Nana."

And I'd say, "I know I don't have to. You are a good boy and I do it because I love you."

Promises made long ago are promises to keep.

WHAT DO I DO NOW?
2002

I picked up the phone in Oregon and heard my 4-year-old grandson, Nick, sobbing in Arizona.

I said, "Nick, what is the matter? Honey, try to calm down and tell Nana what's wrong?"

"Nana, I want you to come home. I want you to be here now!"

"Is your momma there?"

Through his tears, he said, "She's in the kitchen."

"Just let me talk to her for a minute and I'll come back to you, okay?"

He handed the phone to his mom.

I said, "Alicia, did you put Nick up to this?"

"No, mom, he was upset when he woke up and was talking about wanting you to be here."

"Okay, let me talk to him again and see if I can make him feel better."

She gave him the phone and I explained that I wanted to see him, too, and that he and his mom would be coming to visit me in Oregon soon. We would have a good time. He seemed to calm down. We said I love you and hung up. I felt shaken by the conversation.

I called my dad who had fourteen grandchildren and asked, "If you don't bond with your grandkids when they are little, do you ever?"

He said with certainty, "Nope."

I told my partner, Ray, about it at dinner. He asked," Would you rather be near your family?"

"Yes, but I have just gotten this bed and breakfast built. I finally have guests. I do miss my family a lot. I don't know what to think."

The next evening at dinner he handed me a letter he had written while on a break at work telling me he'd always dreamed of living in Arizona. I was surprised.

I talked with my daughter, Alicia, the next day. I asked how she would feel about us moving to Arizona. She said it would be great for her kids to have their Nana nearby and for us all to be together. I missed her, my sons, daughter- in law, and the grand-kids. Everyone was in Arizona except me. My partner and I decided moving was the right thing to do.

Within six months, Alicia and Nick spotted the perfect house near them the same day it went on the market. We closed a deal to buy it that evening. My partner, Ray, got a job he really wanted in nearby Flagstaff. I sold my bed and breakfast. It all seemed meant to be.

I am so grateful Alicia dialed the phone for Nick that day.

🔑 **The needs of a child can change your whole life.**

FAMILY,
LOVE AND
RELATIONSHIPS

GRANDMA'S RING

1945

Grandma's life had been hard. She divorced her alcoholic husband when my mother was twelve years old. They lived in places where my Grandma could find a job as a housekeeper. Mom didn't remember having a home of their own.

After Mom graduated from high school at eighteen, she went to work for the phone company. It was the end of World War II, 1945. At that time, Grandma was dating a man, Cass, whose nineteen-year-old nephew, Dean, was coming home on a thirty day leave from his naval base in California to Michigan.

He had just returned from his tour in the Pacific. Grandma thought he'd be a great date for my mom, Marcia, and it turned out he was. When Dean got to town, the four of them went out dancing and the flame was lit! Marcia and the handsome sailor saw each other every night he was in town.

Dean had to return to California to finish the process of getting out of the service. He called Marcia every night while he was gone. After five weeks of phone calls, he asked her to come to California on the train to marry him. She immediately said, "Yes!"

When she got off the phone, she went to Grandma and told her, "I am going to California to marry Dean." Grandma had enough experience with marriage and divorce to know you had to be very sure before you took the leap. Divorce had made her life terribly difficult. She said adamantly, "Oh, no. You're not going to go off like that so suddenly!"

"Oh, yes I am!" This went back and forth until Grandma realized Marcia's mind was made up. She sat down with her daughter and presented her with a wedding ring.

"It was mine," she said. "I've kept it for you. You should have it in case Dean doesn't have one. I think you know how I feel about this marriage, but I have faith in you."

Marcia asked, "What's gotten you through the tough times, Mom? What advice do you have for me?" as she admired the ring.

"I do worry, of course. Going so far away and marrying after such a short time together. I'd be lying if I didn't tell you I'm concerned for you."

"No. No. This is what I want," Marcia said earnestly. "It'll be fine. I love the idea of living in the California sunshine. I'll find a good job. We'll be so happy! And this ring makes it perfect." She was glowing.

"You're a good girl," Grandma said, with tears in her eyes. "I'll miss you. The best advice that's worked for me is to do the best you can with what you know, at the time you know it, in good conscience, then no regrets."

Cass, who became my great uncle, gave Marcia $100 for her trip to California.

Within a week, Grandma hugged Marcia warmly before she got on the train.

When she got to California, Dean had a wedding and engagement ring. Marcia wore the ring from Grandma as well, and never took any of them off. Mom shared Grandma's advice with me and I use it often.

🗝 **Wisdom and gifts from our mothers and grandmothers may be treasures beyond measure.**

ACCEPTANCE

1975

It was 1975 in Phoenix, Arizona. I was sitting at my kitchen table. I was proud of the fact that my first attempt at wall papering with a cute red and white checkered pattern came out so well. There were matching red and white cotton curtains on the kitchen window over the sink and a red table cloth on the table. It looked cheerful. And I was pleased.

I held the phone to my ear in another intense conversation with my sister, Jan. Once again we were debating about her desire that I be saved by accepting Jesus Christ as my Savior. She had recently been saved at a Billy Graham crusade at Arizona State University stadium. She was ecstatic about her new life and wanted to convince me that I needed to be saved also or I was going to hell.

She said, "Deni, you won't believe how it will change everything to have Jesus as your Savior."

"How does getting saved work?"

"Well, you would come to our Baptist Church service. Near the end of the service the pastor makes a request that anyone interested in having Jesus Christ as their Savior come forward. The next step is to schedule a time to be baptized by being dunked underwater in the baptismal at the church."

I said, "Well, I've already been baptized at the Methodist Church we were raised in."

"No. That's not a real baptism because you were just sprinkled. That doesn't count. It won't keep you from going to hell. Only those who've accepted Jesus Christ will be saved. That's why I want this for you."

I asked, "How do you know this for sure?"

"I know because it's written in the Bible. Everything you need to know about life is written in the Bible."

At this point I was feeling pretty pressured and said, "You mean everything I need to know in life is in the Bible?"

"Yes."

"Well, I don't see electricity in the Bible and we use it every day." Oohhh.... that felt terrible. Suddenly I realized I'd gone too far. I apologized and said we needed to stop this debate. I didn't want to lose my sister.

"Do you believe in your heart of hearts that this faith is making you truly happy?"

"Yes," she said.

"Well, I am so glad that you have found this new faith. I accept that. I, too, have spiritual beliefs that make me very happy. Could you give me the same grace?"

She agreed right then to stop trying to change my beliefs. Although, she said, "I will still pray for you."

I thanked her for that. We decided not to discuss religion again for a while and we have been very close for many years.

🗝 **Acceptance of different philosophies helps sustain loving, long lasting relationships.**

SILENT AND SECRET

1976

I thought it was all my fault. I found the note on the bedroom dresser on Saturday morning, the day before Mother's Day. I'd just brought our kids, aged nine, six and four, back home from swimming at Grandma's. The note from my husband, Tim, said, "I need to get away for a while", so I figured he'd gone shopping or for a drive.

He called at 5:30 that late afternoon and said, "I'm not coming back."

I didn't get it. I asked, "What do you mean you're not coming back?"

"I'm not coming home and I quit my job." Silence.

After thirteen years our marriage was over? I couldn't take it in. This wasn't really happening! But even through the shock, I knew it was. I hung up the phone, stunned, and sank into a nearby chair. What would happen to the kids? We'd agreed to give the kids a full-time mom. I hadn't worked in seven years and only knew how to type and file. And now, my husband said he had quit his job, as well as his family all in the same day! We had just moved into our new house ten months before. Suddenly, we had no income, no health benefits or savings. All I could imagine was that I would lose our house, end up in the ghetto and my kids would be juvenile delinquents. That night I cried my heart out.

The next morning I knew I needed help thinking through what had happened. I arranged to see my college counselor, Charlie, that afternoon. We sat in his book-filled office, and I tearfully told my story.

"What is he like?" he asked. Charlie was a kind, middle-aged, divorced father of four. He seemed calm and wise.

"Oh, he's the silent type—intelligent, hard-working, a good dad, sometimes a procrastinator."

"Anything else?" he said looking out the window at the desert landscape and college buildings. I hoped he would be able to tell me how to save my marriage, save the dream.

"Well..." I began, "when I approach him with problems, he doesn't want to deal with them. When I ask how he feels, he says, 'I don't know.' No matter how I try, nothing changes."

"I see," Charlie said. He leaned forward toward me. "Do you understand that the person who will not speak has all the power?"

All of a sudden I realized what had been going on during our thirteen year marriage. My husband's silence kept me completely alone. In that moment I felt liberated from self-blame and guilt. I was filled with a new sense of determination.

Be wary of choosing a partner who is unable to communicate and unwilling to get help.

FINDING GOOD FORTUNE

1977

I t was the Arizona summer of 1977. I was thirty one years old and newly separated from my husband. I sold Indian jewelry, baskets and rugs to support myself and my three kids, trying to make a go of it. My husband had moved in with his girlfriend. He couldn't afford a divorce and neither could I, but I needed a divorce to give me the financial help that child support would provide.

One of my selling trips was to Tucson in the heat of July. I had told my friend Sybil, who lived there, that I was coming down to see some of my customers. She invited me to her home for the night. I gratefully accepted because I barely had enough money for gas to go there and back.

When I arrived at her place, I saw desert landscaping with cactus showing off deep pink blooms near the front door. She graciously invited me in, gave me a tall glass of ice-cold sun tea, and showed me around her small Mexican adobe home with red tile floors. It felt cool and welcoming.

After catching up on our lives, she said, "I would like you to meet my boyfriend, Mark. I told him about some of the items you were bringing and he said he was interested in seeing them for his office. He offered to take us out for dinner tonight. Would you like to go?"

I said, "That sounds wonderful."

We met Mark at a popular Mexican restaurant. He was an attorney, tall and slim, dark-haired, an attractive guy. He greeted me with a warm, firm handshake and a great smile. After being seated, we ordered our meal, and he asked me how things were going in my life.

During our conversation, I discovered that he already knew a little of my story because Sybil had shared some of it with him. Then we talked about the items I was selling. He seemed interested in the rugs, especially, and asked if I could bring them down to his office the next morning.

I found his office and brought in four of the finest rugs. He decided on an 8x10 rug with the traditional Navajo pattern in red and black colors for his waiting room and another smaller rug with the Navajo corn maiden pattern in black and green for his office. They would look perfect on the rustic wooden floor that matched his Southwestern oak desk and leather furniture.

Then we discussed the price. He said, "I know that you are in a difficult financial situation, and I would be willing to work an exchange of these two rugs for the cost of your divorce, if you'd like."

I was stunned and could hardly believe my good fortune! "Well, that would be wonderful. I accept your offer."

Mark educated me about divorce and child support. I had no idea what was involved. By his calculations, I was entitled to $250.00 per child per month. Then he asked me, "Which of your regular bills are you the most concerned about?"

"The house payment," I said.

"How much is that?"

"It's $375 a month."

While running his hand over the rug with the corn maiden pattern, he asked the most important question. "Do you want what the court will say you deserve, or do you want what your husband is likely to pay?" That was an eye opener.

The amount of $375 a month would break down to $125 per month per child. It was less than I deserved, but my ex-husband would likely be able to pay me every month. I wasn't interested in chasing down my ex-husband for money he couldn't pay. He had a job in a tool and die shop, didn't make much income, but was a steady worker. I wanted a fair allotment that he could afford.

I also wanted peace in our relationship. The kids needed a father and mother who could get along. If my ex-husband could make regular payments, I would be able to manage my life somehow and keep a roof over our heads, I hoped.

"Bless you!" I said to Mark as we closed our deal. The divorce was completed within six months and I was able to start a new life.

🗝 **Get a kind and trustworthy expert on your side when you need help.**

CAN YOU HEAR ME NOW?

2003

That thought crossed her mind unexpectedly, when she and her husband were having an argument about how to restore a second bathroom.

He asked, "How do you want the shower changed?"

She said, "I want the shower in the right corner. It will make more space in the room."

He ignored her and replied, "I am going to put the cabinets in the right corner with the sinks next to them. The shower will go on the left."

He was not listening! She said, "I'm either going to teach you or hate you.

Which would you like?" What she meant was would you listen to me when I give you an answer and not ignore what I've said?

He is fourteen years older than she is, comes from the old-fashioned training of how men deal with women, and he was not paying attention to her. She was attempting to communicate with some humor and, yet, she meant it.

He looked at her, slowly smiled and they started the conversation over. The bathroom turned out in a way they both liked and communication between them is better now.

🗝 **Lack of listening, cooperation, and willingness to compromise may create resentment and a loss of love and respect.**

MOM'S HIDDEN THOUGHTS

1980

My mom died of ovarian cancer at age fifty-four. She knew how to manage her life, and she was also in charge of her death. She graduated from Arizona State University with a Master's degree at age fifty-two and was qualified to be a counselor. She could give advice, but she didn't like to take it. We tried to tell her what we thought was best for her which she did not always accept.

When mom's doctor suspected cancer—and told her to see a surgeon right away—she took a six-week camping vacation with my dad instead. She did not tell anyone what the doctor had said. I think mom thought it was important to be with her husband, just the two of them.

The trip had been planned for several months. They had taken very few trips by themselves in their thirty-five years together. I think she went on the trip because she wanted to work on her marriage. They had just finished couple's counseling for the first time. She wasn't willing to change her plans because of the suspected cancer. So they took the trip, and she went into surgery and treatment when they returned.

Mom was also at a stopping point in her life. She said to me one day, "Even though I've got a Master's degree in counseling, I don't see myself deserving to be paid as a counselor nor can I see myself staying with your dad or leaving and living on my own." She felt trapped. It was difficult for her to talk about a future. She never said much about her life after that. I knew her mother had died of ovarian cancer at age fifty-six, and I was worried. If Mom was worried, she didn't show it. I know my father didn't know how she felt, either.

Over the next year and a half, she had treatments, went into remission, and then the cancer came back with a deadly vengeance. At Dad's request, she reluctantly agreed to an experimental drug. It soon raised boils on her skin and was very painful. She requested that the treatment be stopped. The cancer was at its worst and the doctors had no other solution for her.

The family members took turns being with her the rest of her days at the hospital. I took the night shift. One night, she woke out of a coma and told me, "I just want to die. I can see my mother and she will be with me on the other side. Will you be alright?" I said, "I promise I will. It's okay to go, Mom." We both said, "I love you." She closed her eyes, went back into a coma and passed away three days later.

I don't think she regretted the decision to go on vacation with Dad instead of seeing an oncologist right away. It made my heart ache though I understood. It was a relief that her suffering was over.

🗝 **It can be difficult to understand why a person makes the choices they do in their life. May we love them enough to accept their decisions.**

YOU WILL NO LONGER BE THE DECIDER

1990

We weren't having a good time any more. Every conversation became a confrontation. It was all about who was right or wrong or who to blame. It seemed that I could not find a topic to discuss without an argument. If I agreed with him, things seemed just fine. If I disagreed, I was wrong.

Once, I told my partner I felt good about being able give a friend or family member money when they needed help.

"You should be loaning and charging interest, not just giving it away," he said in a condescending voice. The nerve of him! It was my money I was using!

Another time he came home upset about something that had happened at work. I greeted him with a smile and a kiss, and he said, "Do you always have to be so cheerful?"

His responses left me on an emotional roller coaster and it was getting old. It finally occurred to me that I was allowing this type of communication to control my level of happiness. I was taking charge at work. How come I couldn't do that at home?

One fine memorable day I got up the gumption to say, "You will no longer be the determiner of my happiness or unhappiness. From now on, that will be up to me only." His mouth dropped open and he looked stunned.

That insight made me realize that if my partner chose to be unhappy, depressed, argumentative or grumpy, I didn't have to participate. That was his choice, and it wasn't my job to fix him.

🗝 **Another person's frame of mind does not have to determine ours, unless we let it.**

OH, THAT'S
WHAT MATTERS!
1991

Who knew my second husband, Rob, would say something I thought was funny that ended our marriage?

After work, I drove from Phoenix to the construction site in Prescott where Rob was building a home for a client. He was working for himself as a contractor. My work at that time was managing the process of building cell phone stores. Rob thought we would make great partners as we both understood construction. Not so much, it turns out.

He requested my opinion when I arrived. "Would you take a look at this blueprint? I don't like the design of the stairwell to the basement. Have you got a better idea?"

I suggested, "I would make it straight down rather than curved, allowing a cleaner line and more floor space at the bottom."

Angrily, he replied, "Well, that wasn't very bright. I could have figured that out myself." That was enough. I left without responding to him.

Driving to our summer home, I wondered why I was staying in this relationship. I had a good job at a management level, had raised three children as a single mom, and thought I was happy. As long as Rob's needs were our first priority and he could control everything, including me, our marriage seemed to work.

When he got back to the house later, I told him I wanted to talk. He got his usual afternoon rum and coke and settled into the chair across from me. "What did you want to talk about?"

Feeling the inner strength of facing reality that afternoon, gave me the courage to speak my truth. I had never had the confidence or self-respect to end a relationship before.

Surprising even me, I heard myself say, "I deserve to be loved and cherished in a way that feels loving to me. If that's not going to happen here, I have to go."

I waited for his response, thinking he might want to talk over our situation and maybe come to some understanding about how to make things better.

He looked at me and paused as if to collect his thoughts. The biggest shock was his answer. He said, "Can I have my diamond ring back?" I just started laughing. It was instantly clear what really mattered to him.

I replied, "No. I will treasure this ring as a reminder of a lovely romance I once had in my life."

Each of us deserves to feel loved and cherished.

GRANDPA'S UNKNOWN STORY
1989

At age ninety my grandpa was healthy, wore glasses, was clean shaven and had thinning gray hair. He was of medium height and weight. The few times I saw him, he wore a dress shirt and slacks with his shoes always shined. He lived far away in Michigan. My step grandma, Mina, had died fifteen years before and Grandpa was alone at his two acre home. About that time, we started having more chats on the phone. I'd call him from Arizona, not worrying about the cost of the call. Grandpa was frugal and not one to pick up the charges.

I'd always start the conversation by asking, "How are you doing, Grandpa?"

"Well, not as good as I used to." "Oh, hell, Grandpa, no one's doing as good as they used to." And we'd always laugh after our standard greeting.

Seeking his advice I asked, "If you had your life to live over, what would you have done differently?"

"I wish I had travelled more." His deep voice sounded younger than his years.

I asked, "Grandpa, you have more money than God! Why didn't you go?"

"Mina wouldn't pay her half! So, we only went to Mexico once."

I had to cover the mouthpiece and chuckle. I wasn't really surprised. Every year he sent me $5.00 for my birthday. That says it all. Mina had enough of her own money. Prior to meeting Grandpa, she had a successful nursing career, was self-supporting, and had an income from a previous marriage. They could have travelled, but their stubbornness about how to share the cost kept them at home.

Years later, at my grandfather's funeral, an elderly gentleman came up to me and said,

"Are you Pete's granddaughter?" I said, "Yes, I am."

"Well, I worked with your grandfather at Clarke Equipment."

Grandpa left home at fourteen and worked at a mental hospital for a short time. At age sixteen he started working at Clarke Equipment, and retired forty two years later in his hometown of Albion, near Detroit. The plant made small parts for Ford, the auto manufacturer. One day Grandpa told me a favorite story about when he became a superintendent. Each week he would wrap a finished part in a cloth, take it on the train to Detroit and have the quality of the part inspected by a Ford examiner. One day, when he arrived, he was asked to wait in the lobby across from a conference room. In that room he could see a man wearing a white shirt and tie. The man came out and asked Grandpa what he had. Grandpa showed him the part and the man said, "This is very fine work." Grandpa thanked him and the man walked away.

Grandpa asked the receptionist who

that man was and she said, "That was Henry Ford. Not many people get to speak with him."

At Grandpa's funeral this gentleman told me, "I want you to know that during the Depression your grandpa saw to it that no one under his supervision lost their job." Grandpa never told anyone about that. I thanked the gentleman for telling me. It changed my impression of my grandpa from a miserly man to a man who also had a great deal of compassion. He had done a wonderful thing for his employees and their families during a very difficult time.

While living his last few years being cared for by his loving daughter, my Aunt Jean, Grandpa lived to be seven days shy of 100 years of age, passing in 1998. He was healthy, liked his three meals a day, took care of his stock portfolio, and read the paper up to the last day when he closed his eyes after lunch for his afternoon nap and did not wake up.

🔑 **Be careful how you judge a person. Some generosities may be hidden.**

I GOT TO SAY GOODBYE
2009

I got the news at my office in Arizona that afternoon. My father had only about forty-eight hours to live. I left work and cried all the way home. We hadn't seen each other for over a year. Our relationship was broken.

Back when I lived in Oregon, managing my bed and breakfast, my dad would visit and stay in the small cottage next to it. He loved it there. I cooked his favorite meals and took him to his appointments. We were so close for years, but now he was no longer the father I'd known. Someone had convinced my dad that I was a liar.

Dementia had taken away his ability to understand that this was not true. He no longer wanted to see me. It was so sad.

It was time to decide how our last hours would be. Should I drive the hundred miles to see him in the hospital? Would he be angry? Would he want to talk to me? Would he be glad I came? Could we make up, settle things? Should I stay away and not upset him?

When I got home, my partner, Ray, sat at the table with me. After hearing what was going on, he asked, "What do you want to do?"

I said through my tears, "I'm sitting here trying to decide that."

"Do you want a suggestion?" I nodded, and Ray asked, "What will you wish you had done a year from now?"

What a wonderful question! I felt a sense of peace and knew I had to go. It was still frightening, but I had to go. I packed some clothes, not knowing how it would be when I got there. Ray stood waiting at the gate, and we kissed goodbye. He said,

"Remember, even if you are sorry you did this today, a year from now you'll be glad you did."

God bless him. It was true. I'm so glad I got to see my father in his last days. When I got to his bedside, he opened his eyes and asked, "Why are you here?"

I took his hand and said, "I wanted you to know that I love you and that Mom is waiting for you on the other side."

"Why?" he asked.

"Because she loves you, we all love you, Dad."

He closed his eyes and went back to sleep. I kissed his cheek. He died several days later.

Three months after he passed I dreamed Dad was at our house in Arizona. We had finished dinner and he was getting ready to leave. When I hugged him good-bye, as I always did, his eyes filled with tears. I asked him what was the matter, and he asked, "Can I stay the night?" I said, "Certainly you can."

The next night after dinner, he pre-pared to leave again, and after my hug he tearfully asked, "Can I stay forever?" "Of course you can." I hugged him and woke up.

I am so grateful for that dream and the peace it gave me.

With love, time can heal everything.

HURT PEOPLE
HURT PEOPLE
1989

My friend, Kathleen, attended a Sid Simon Seminar on forgiveness and was quite moved by the experience. She told me of the phrase, *hurt people, hurt people*"—how people who've been hurt can readily hurt others. It reminded me of my friend, Scott, who sometimes spoke sarcastically and offended people.

Recently he and his wife, Carole, had joined us along with other mutual friends at our cabin in New Mexico. Scott and I were getting to know each other. One afternoon, as we were sitting outdoors on the sunny deck, Scott asked me how it was going at my job where I'd been having a hard time.

"Not great," I said. "Lots of expecta-tions, not enough time; too many people to keep on task."

"Sounds like you've got a boss who's unrealistic," Scott said. "If I were you—."

I interrupted him with more com-plaints, and he said sharply, "Thank you for interrupting me."

I was stunned, hurt, and tears welled up.

"Sorry," he muttered as he jumped up and went inside.

Later that evening Scott and I were on opposite ends of a couch in the living room talking after dinner. Scott didn't seem to be a very warm person, but he was bright and a good conversationalist. I was deciding whether I liked him or not. As he launched into another subject, I must have interrupt-ed, because he said, "Thanks for interrupt-ing me once again!"

"How does it serve you to be so sarcas-tic?" I snapped back.

And he flashed right back at me, "I don't know, but I'm working on it."

I think it was in that moment we became friends. Our friendship grew, and about six months later, at his home in front of a big beautiful fireplace, we had one of our great discussions. I was able to ask him about his past, especially his childhood. I learned that he'd been badly abused. "Do you think that may be why you're so sarcastic?" I asked.

"Who knows?" he said.

I shared what I'd learned from Kathleen and asked, "Is it possible you fall into the group of hurt people who hurt people?"

Scott looked shocked and said nothing.

Later he was able to tell me that my question was a powerful insight for him and had changed his life.

Knowing someone's painful past allows an opportunity for understanding and compassion.

KINDRED SPIRITS

2004

N ow and then I meet someone I feel I've known forever. This happened to me one time at a writing seminar. There were many writers, students, and intellectuals there in the large hotel—a FASCINATING crowd. It was my job to capture the author's presentation on DVD for use later at the community college.

As people were finishing up their refreshments at the break, I saw this six foot tall, slender woman with shoulder length gray hair. She moved gracefully across the lobby, and I found her intriguing. She seemed to know many of the people in the room. I noticed her easy way of meeting everyone and assumed she was a professor from the college.

I dutifully did the recording, attended some of the talks, and found everything offered at the event captivating. I had a dream of writing a book. Here was information I needed. It seemed entirely serendipitous that I would be in a room with nationally known published authors, soaking up everything said and taking careful notes.

The first night of my Gerontology class back at the college the following week, I saw the intriguing woman again. She, too, was a student in the class and we said hello at the break. She said she had noticed me that night at the hotel, too. She seemed a little shy as we talked, and I was surprised after seeing her so at ease at the seminar.

As the weeks progressed, she opened up. During our class breaks we went to the college cafeteria to get a snack and chatted about attending college as adults, our families, and the gerontology topics that were raised in the class. To me, it felt as if we'd known each other a long time, though she seemed different from anyone else I'd ever met.

I began to notice the mental shorthand going on between us. We'd complete each other's sentences and seemed to easily grasp what the other was thinking or feeling. It was a gift to find someone who had a funny, off beat sense of humor, keen insights and a different point of view.

How does this happen? Are there people we are destined to find? I now know what 'kindred spirit' means and I'm grateful.

The feeling of having known someone before could signal a dear friendship.

COAT OF NAILS
2004

I was putting together binders for our next meeting. The room was cluttered with stacks of papers on each table, but I knew where everything was. I had to organize these clunky binders for fifty people, but I rather enjoyed being away from my desk, having quiet time to myself while doing a simple task.

The summer season made the asphalt outside our window look ready to melt. Arizona dry heat took no prisoners. I was glad to be inside where it was cool and comfortable.

Kate came in and wanted me to stop working and listen to her. She was upset, and she'd been that way ever since I'd known her. The reason was the terrible loss of her sixteen-year-old son six years before. He had died of leukemia, and she had never recovered from his death. She kept his picture on the screen saver on her computer and showed it, tearfully, to everyone who passed by her desk. She'd been seeing counselors and took medication but was having difficulty moving on with her life.

Today she left her station to seek me out for comfort again. She asked me, "Deni, what do you think I should do? I'm in such pain!" And she started to cry.

I wondered what in the world I could say that would help. Then out of my mouth came, "Well, Kate, it seems you wear your sadness like a coat of nails. When the opportunity comes to tell the story again, you pull the coat closer to you and re-live the pain." Where did that come from? It had popped out of my mouth without warning.

I felt horrified that I'd spoken so frankly! Coat of nails? I waited for her hysterics, but there was silence.

Then she said, "It's true. It feels like nails in my body."

"Do you think your son would want you to be living your life this way?" I asked, still wondering if I had hurt her.

She shook her head, her dark hair a halo around her face, but she wasn't crying.

"I'll tell you what I think," I said. "I believe you have the strength to overcome your loss."

After a moment, she pulled me into a hug and quietly left.

I went back to my binders, silently praying for peace and tranquility in her life.

Sometimes speaking truthfully is the most kindhearted response.

SPECIAL PANCAKES

2010

My son, Adam, had invited me to his house for the weekend. I woke up Sunday to a beautiful, sunny morning. The delicious smell of bacon was in the air. Then I knew Adam had gotten up early to make pancakes, eggs and fruit for me, his wife, Jill, and his kids, Chance and Shianne. His brother, Andy, was on his way over to eat with us as well as his sister, Alicia and her two sons, Nick and Josh.

As I entered the kitchen, I said, "Boy, it sure smells good in here."

Adam said, "Good morning. Your tea is all made in the pot on the table."

"You are such a thoughtful guy."

He spread the batter in the pan and watched over the little cakes, turning them just as the bubbles popped. He enjoyed cooking, especially for family, and knew we loved his tasty homemade pancakes.

Andy, Alicia and the boys arrived and Adam served his breakfast piping hot. I said to him, "I'll wait until the others are finished, then we'll eat together." Everyone commented on how good it all tasted. Adam and Andy gave each other the usual humorous jabs, and we all laughed. Jill, Alicia and the grandkids gave us an update on what was new with them. I thought to myself, "This is what I treasure, having them all in the same room and listening to their stories."

When everyone else had finished, Adam served up our plates and sat down with me at the table. Now sweet Jill—who likes things tidy—quickly began cleaning up the dirtied dishes and was loading them into the dishwasher. Next she wiped up the counters and the stove.

Adam and I had just buttered our pan-cakes when she arrived at the table with sponge in hand. She reached for the syr-up bottle to put it away when Adam said gently, "Jill, we haven't finished with the syrup or our breakfast yet. Mom and I are going to take our time eating. I know you want things cleaned up. I'll take care of that when we're done. Don't worry. It's just your nature and we love you just the way you are."

🗝 **Everyone has their own way of doing things. Unconditional love makes room for those differences.**

THE COWBOY
2003

I call my sister, Jan, the Erma Bombeck of the family. Her little lines of wisdom come out in our conversations and we laugh. I ask her if she's writing them down. She says she doesn't have to because I am. We had been talking about what happens in a marriage when the "glow" wears off. It's that old taken-for-granted routine that some of us know so well. She said that her husband, like most men, doesn't want to hear a long complaint, so she comes up with these short, witty ways of getting her message across. Like, "If a woman doesn't feel pretty, a man's not being a man," is about a shortage of compliments.

He is a manly cowboy and gets her meaning. One of their secrets seems to be the humor they share.

On another occasion the cowboy came to the kitchen door. Jan was at the sink loading the new dishwasher. He said to her "I think we save more money by hand washing the dishes instead of using that machine. It uses more electricity and more water." For her it brought up too many frustrations. He wasn't thinking of the convenience for her, what he said was not sensible, and she didn't want to get into an argument with him over it. So, she turned to him and said, "Who are you and what have you done with my husband?" They broke up laughing.

Comedy can smooth out the bumpy spots in a relationship.

WHAT'S THE MARTYR WITH YOU

1987

My friend Sue and her husband, Harold, planned for a nice dinner out with dancing afterwards to celebrate their first date thirty seven years before. She even bought a pretty lavender blouse to wear with her long deep purple full skirt. Her face glowed with a smile as she told me how much she was looking forward to it.

The morning of the dinner, Sue's son, Richard, called and said, "Mom, we need a babysitter tonight. Tammy and I have an important business dinner with my boss and his wife. Our babysitter just called and cancelled. I am sorry to call on such short notice.

Can you please help us out?"

Her son and family lived a few blocks away. It didn't occur to Sue to ask her husband if it was alright with him, she just said, "Of course we can. Just bring the kids over for dinner with us. I have pajamas for them. They can spend the night here, if you like."

When she hung up the phone, she went out on the porch and told her husband that they wouldn't be going out to dinner. She told him how disappointed she was. When she explained why they had to cancel, he was not happy and said sternly, "Did you ask him if he had tried to get in touch with another sitter? Did you tell him we had plans tonight?"

In a whiny voice she said, "Well no, Harold, I didn't. You know the kids need me to help them out. I just can't say no."

Sue had a history of doing for others because she said she had to, not because she wanted to. When she told stories of those times, she'd say, "Well, it was really inconvenient, but what else could I do? They needed me."

We all know someone like that, don't we?

Two days later she told me the story about cancelling her dinner with her husband.

I asked, "So what's the martyr with you?" Sue looked a little hurt by that, but I went on to say, "Don't you feel manipulated by your kids for taking advantage of you that way?"

"Well, yes, maybe, but they need me."

I said, "My family and I have an understanding. They will not do anything for me out of obligation and I won't do anything out of obligation for them either. That way we are doing for each other because we want to not because we feel we have to. I like to think our relationship is open and honest in that way."

I've learned that martyrdom is just not healthy. It seems to lead to more anxieties and despair every time. When I hear those stories now, I think, *"Pack your bags, we're going on a guilt trip!"*

🗝 **Doing things we really don't want to do is insincere, builds resentment and can lead to unnecessary harm in relationships.**

SPIRITUALITY

INNER VOICE
1979

My intuition has served me well. It comes to me like an instinctive answer to any question or situation I find perplexing. It seems to be there as a source of wisdom.

I hear that quiet voice, even as my logical mind argues—giving "sensible" answers. It's like two different people debating inside me.

When my logical mind says, "What will people think?" Intuition says, "Listen to me."

When my logical mind says, "That doesn't make any sense," Intuition says, "Listen to me."

Having two points of view inside was frustrating until I asked my Inner Wisdom to turn up the volume. Often the logical point of view tried to take over the intuitive view. This caused confusion even though I had been helped by those little messages. I wanted to make sure they weren't ignored when the critical, logical point of view tried to negate them.

I spoke to a counselor about the dueling voices. She said, "If you follow your feelings and listen to that whisper, you will likely make the right choice."

When I was working out problems, becoming more aware of my intuition and not ignoring it turned out to be the most successful approach. The more I listened, the clearer the answer became. I'd know the next right thing to do or say.

Over time, I noticed that when someone was telling me a story, I would often see a word or picture in my mind's eye. Sometimes I didn't understand how that word or picture fit the situation, but if I told the person what I was seeing, it seemed to clarify the issue.

Martha came to me for life coaching. She told me her husband suddenly died from a stroke a year and a half before and many of her friends had told her she would feel better after a year had gone by. Instead, at the end of the first year she was more depressed than ever. As she was telling me this, the word "numb" came to my mind. When I asked Martha if that word meant anything to her, she started to cry and said, "Oh, my gosh. I think numb is exactly what I have been feeling. I haven't cried for all this time to avoid the pain. I'm just now beginning to feel the reality and sadness of my loss."

The heightened awareness of the importance of this gift allows me to use my intuition almost daily to help myself and others.

Trusting and listening may lead to answers we might never have considered.

JESUS AT
THE MOVIES
2004

.

I was in a movie theater sitting on the far right aisle about halfway from the stage. The drapes were pulled back and there was a full screen view of Jesus Christ. He then stepped out of the screen, walked across the stage and down the steps, up the right-hand aisle toward me.

He stopped at my seat and looked down at me with the most loving eyes, then touched my shoulder. I felt an incredible vibrating glow inside my body. How loved and powerful it made feel is indescribable.

Jesus said to me, "You have this power and can show others how they have it, too."

I turned to the person next to me to say that the power wasn't just for me, it was for everyone. I had to share the wonderful moment.

Then I saw other people in the theater begin to light up. When I turned back to Jesus, he had disappeared. I woke up, but I have a clear memory of the dream I've kept in my heart.

We all have the power of grace and goodness within us. Remember to share it.

SHE FOUND A WAY

1981

My mother and I had read the book, *A World Beyond* by Ruth Montgomery, a year before she knew she had cancer. The book describes what happens in the afterlife. It contained messages Montgomery received from her friend, the famous medium, Arthur Ford, after he died.

Mom and I were intrigued. Ford had written about levels of learning after death, and we talked a lot about it. What if this idea about the afterlife was true? What if there was a world beyond this one? After Mom learned that she had cancer, and that it had reached the terminal stage, she and I made a pact. If she could reach me from the other side, as we believed possible, she would.

After her death, I visited Jan, my friendly psychic. She was nearly six feet tall, wore her red hair in a beehive and had a wonderful deep laugh. It had been several months since Mom's passing and I wondered if Jan would share anything about Mom's life on the other side.

After she finished my reading, Jan asked, "Any other questions, Deni?" She smiled and leaned back in her chair. I was disappointed that she had not mentioned anything about my mother!

"Where's my mother?" I asked.

Jan got quiet, closed her eyes and waited. In a few moments she said, "I see a huge field of yellow and white flowers. There's a large house with a front porch. Your mother is sitting in a rocking chair there....."

I thought to myself, *Oh brother, she's going to tell me my mother's in South Carolina.*

"Has anyone in your family lost a child?" Jan inquired.

I thought a few moments and said, "No."

"Are you sure?"

"Why are you asking?"

"There's a boy standing next to your mother's chair. He's about four years old."

Oh my God! I remembered that my cousin had terminated a pregnancy four years ago and mom wondered what happened to the soul of that baby. She was showing me the answer. I was amazed!

Then Jan's voice changed and said, "I am fine and very happy. I go to school every day (another answer). I love you and will be with you when you need me."

I felt an electrical charge all through me. That was my mother's voice.

🗝 **Contact made. Belief in an afterlife confirmed.**

MIRACLES

1982

After my divorce, I'd found a job as an accounting clerk but this month I was not going to be able to make the $156.00 car payment. I had no credit, there was no one who could loan it to me, and I couldn't have paid it back anyway.

I told the Universe, "I need help. I've tried everything and come up empty."

The next day I found a check for $157.50 in my mailbox. It was made out to me. I never questioned its origin, just cashed it and made the payment. A miracle.

Then, the week before Christmas, the company I worked for went bankrupt, and the entire staff was laid off.

Worse, I was facing a needed surgery in January. I was so scared. What was I going to do now?

That very evening, an old friend and neighbor, Bill, called and asked me to come see his new real estate office nearby. I hadn't seen him in quite a while. Our history together included my helping him survive after his wife suddenly left him.

When I arrived, he locked the door and showed me around his beautifully decorated office. Then I sat down in a soft leather chair across from his mahogany desk to catch up on our lives. Bill sensed something was wrong. "What's bothering you, Deni?" he asked.

"I'm okay," I lied.

"I'm not unlocking the door until you tell me what's wrong," he insisted.

"I'll tell you, but after that I don't want to talk about it," I said, feeling anxious and upset. "I've lost my stupid job, can't afford a needed surgery and don't know what I'm going to do." I looked down at my shoes, humiliated and trying not to cry.

"How much are your monthly expenses?" I told him. He continued, "I'm so sorry about what's happened. I'll keep an eye out for a job for you." Changing the subject, he asked, "Would you meet me at the bank tomorrow morning? I need some financial advice." Being at the bank with him was not an unusual request. I had helped him set up a business in the past.

"I guess I have plenty of time for that," I said bitterly. The next morning I drove into the city to meet Bill at the bank. It seemed odd that the bank officer greeted me by my formal name. When Bill arrived, we sat down at the bank officer's desk and he pushed a paper toward us that had my name on it. It was a loan, co-signed by Bill, which would cover all my expenses for six months.

I was shocked!

Bill turned to me, as I sputtered my questions, and he told me, "I made the amount enough so you'd have time to recover from your surgery and find a new job."

He seemed so pleased to help, and I remembered when he'd been in need and I was able to help him. Another miracle!

🔑 **I trust that the Universe is conspiring on my behalf even when I can't see it.**

PLAN B

1982

I was fired? What? I'd never been fired from a job in my life! I was the over achiever, the one who would get work done faster and more efficiently than anyone else. But this time I'd been set up. Having been hired to be an administrative assistant with some payroll duties, I was shocked on my first day to be seated at the desk of the former purchasing agent.

I said to the office manager, "There must be some mistake. This isn't what I was hired to do." The response was, "We need this position filled first and you can learn how to do it."

I then realized I had been misled. Without any training or assistance on how to be a purchasing agent, I floundered for six weeks and was then fired with no notice or severance pay. I was stunned, but then relieved to be out of the nightmare that sent me home crying in frustration every night.

I thought to myself, how do I find another job that would pay enough to support me and my three kids? I looked in the newspaper ads, dressed every day for interviews for any job, and after ten days without any luck, I was afraid. I had no savings, groceries were running low, and money for gas was disappearing.

Out of total desperation, I decided to try my Plan B. I'd call Jeri at the employment agency. I'd met her at one of my previous jobs and we got along well. We set a time to meet the next morning. When I arrived, I saw that Jeri had cracked her door open and was interviewing someone. When she heard me come in, she leaned over and said, "My receptionist is out sick today. I will be with you shortly."

The door stayed slightly open, and I heard Jeri suggest that her client have an interview at the largest company in town. She was reluctant to do so. What I wouldn't give for a job there! I'd applied with them a few days before but was pretty certain that my papers were round-filed and never looked at. Hundreds of people wanted a job there.

Finally Jeri's client agreed to an appointment, but Jeri had trouble getting through to the personnel office at the company. I could hear the number she had to repeat three times to an operator who was trying to assist her. By the third time, I wrote down the number on a matchbook cover in my purse. I knew I shouldn't do it, but I was at my wit's end. Jeri gave up trying to call, and her client said she just wasn't interested and left.

Jeri called me in, and after I took a typing test, she offered me the same job. I asked, "How much does it pay?" When she told me what it was, I said, "I have three kids to support and I need a higher salary. She said, "Well, with your job skills I don't have anything in the range you need." I thanked her for her time and made a beeline for home.

Pulling the matchbook cover out of my purse, I called the number at that company and made an appointment for an interview. The secretary who was helping me asked, "How did you get this number?" I answered, "One of the people I bowl with works at this company," which was true. Less than a week later I was called on my birthday and learned I had successfully negotiated the higher salary I needed and got the job.

Keep the faith, don't give up, and your goal will be met.

T.A.N.A.
1993

Kathleen called me on a Sunday morning and invited me to go to a spiritual event that afternoon. I'd been searching for some instruction on how to meditate. Maybe this would be the place.

"There'll be a fascinating speaker, I understand," Kathleen said. "She teaches a method of accessing our inner knowing."

"That suits me," I said. 'What perfect timing."

We drove to a lovely small church in Scottsdale. Its grounds were landscaped with cactus, boulders, and ocotillo shoots topped in slender red blossoms.

Inside we found the room where we would hear the lecture. A horseshoe-shaped array of tables was set in the back with different kinds of materials that offered information about psychic healing, Reiki, mediums, crystals, and the reading of palms etc. I was fascinated! Bob, a friend of Kathleen's, stood at the very last table. He was handing out materials on meditation classes. Delighted, I shook his hand, and he told me he was a psychologist specializing in Gestalt Therapy. He was a handsome man with a warm, quiet demeanor, and his classes sounded like just what I was looking for. I took his information, and Kathleen and I found seats together.

When the time came to introduce the speaker, Bob stood on the small stage and shared his twenty years of experience as a student of spiritual studies. Then he said, "I began to wonder what my own spiritual stories were. The speaker I am about to introduce has been my mentor. She taught me how to access my own inner knowing." I leaned forward to try and catch a glimpse of the mystery guest.

A young man came up to Bob and whispered in his ear. Then Bob said, "I have some bad news. The speaker has had a threat against her life, and she will not be presenting today. You can collect your refund at the door. I thought to myself, "I'm so disappointed." Just then Kathleen turned to me and wrote on my sleeve with her finger the letters T.A.N.A., our shorthand for *There Are No Accidents*.

Of course she was right. What I was really there for was to find Bob and learn about his lessons on meditation, which did open me up to more of my inner knowing.

Our wishes may be granted in unexpected ways.

BENDING TIME
1996

I needed to get to the airport in thirty minutes or would miss my flight home to Phoenix for Christmas. I wasn't the only person who wanted to get home for the holidays. Many folks were scrambling to get to somewhere.

I got in the car and looked at the clock, knowing I was late. I thought, *Okay, I need help bending time or I'll never make it.*

There were four lanes of busy traffic. *Not to worry*, I told myself. *Visualize moving swiftly and easily through it all. This will work!*

My car glided along, "swiftly and easily,"

as if the other drivers were making room for me. There was no trouble getting to the airport in time.

But there was a huge backup of cars trying to get into the airport parking lots! The lanes were solid with congestion. I continued to visualize the slowing of time and a path opening up for me.

Just then a police officer showed up in front of my stopped car and sent me on a new route around the backed-up traffic—leading directly to the rental agency where I needed to drop off my car. *Amazing!*

The hands on my watch seemed to move slowly enough for me to drop off the car, grab my luggage and cross the street right at the entrance to my airline. *It's working!*

When I reached the baggage check-in there was no line.

At the gate they were boarding the last two passengers. I walked onto the plane and took my seat just before the door closed.

After I arranged my brief case and purse, I leaned back, closed my eyes and thanked the Invisible Guidance which helped my journey go smoothly. *Wow!*

Playing with the concept of time on this earth can be fun.

MY ENGLISH ROSE
1997

We were at a garage sale near my California home.

"Yes, I am buying that pretty little creamer," I said.

My partner, Dan, frowned at me. "What are you going to do with all this old stuff you buy?"

"I'm going to put it in the big house," I said. I was so sure of myself that afternoon.

"What big house?" Now he looked surprised.

"I don't know, exactly, but some day I'm going to have a big house in a pretty place."

My dream of a big house wasn't a driving force in life; it just hung around in the back of my mind and was romantic to think about. I'm sure Dan thought it was a pipe dream, but it wasn't.

A few years later, when the kids were raised and I had retired, I visited my sister on the coast of Oregon. I kept imagining a big house with wonderful huge trees around it, the smell of salt sea air and walks on the nearby beaches. It was so heavenly there in Oregon. I was enchanted, in a fairy tale.

Relaxing in my sister's living room the next day, I glanced at the newspaper ads next to me on the couch. The first ad in the real estate column had a picture of a house that looked perfect!

I called the realtor, Van, and he took me to see the house—and twenty other places. Nothing captivated me like the first house I'd seen in the paper. Van and I went back there to look again. It needed some work.

I stood for a while on the one acre property, soaked in the setting, and imagined the house with a wraparound porch. In my view I could see a 1930's drawbridge opening up to allow fishing and sail boats to go down the river, out toward the sun setting on the ocean. There were many tall evergreen trees and room to plant a half acre flower garden with various fragrant English roses, purple hydrangeas, red and yellow dahlias, white calla lilies, and more.

This was not Arizona, where I'd previously lived. This was a piece of green, fertile, beautiful Oregon. I couldn't resist. I would be a new person here in a pretty, inviting home where my little creamer and antique collection would fit perfectly.

I purchased my dream and began the process of remodeling.

Always believing in our dreams brings us everything we need to make them come true.

SHERRY
1998

It was time to visit my ninety-three-year-old friend, Sherry, in Arizona. She greeted me at the door with her warm smile, white wavy hair, a little lipstick and dressed in her matching burgundy pantsuit with a fun necklace of multiple colors. I would bend over to hug her small five foot slim frame. I was always delighted to be with her at her lovely apartment.

Her living room was decorated tastefully with beautiful crystal holding fresh cuts roses, books on her bookshelf which I loved to browse through and paintings she had collected on her travels. Her kitchen table was set with china for our lunch, with tea brewing in a pot and she always lit a candle. When we sat down, she poured our tea and we began. We said a little prayer while holding hands, and then she would ask, "What shall we talk about today?"

From those endearing conversations I received knowledge and insights that changed my life. A few of them are:

When I was overwhelmed with being responsible for many people and situations, she said, "The most loving thing we do for others is to take loving good care of ourselves. If we did that there might be fewer burdens falling on the shoulders of loved ones, co-workers, even countries."

Another sweet time in 1994 with Sherry, she gave me a beautiful small pottery candle holder with a matching tiny plate beneath it, designed in the shape and colors of a flower. I said, "Oh, how pretty! Thank you so much."

She said, "I didn't give it to you because it's pretty. I gave it to you to remind you to keep it light and light hearted."

She told me once, "Heart energy is eight times stronger than the mind."

Also, "If it doesn't make sense, it's not mine."

And one of my favorites, "Peace comes when life can be viewed not as 'good' or 'bad', 'right' or 'wrong', but rather as simply interesting."

I am reminded how grateful I am to Sherry for our lively discussions, laughter, and her kind wisdom over the twenty five years we shared.

Life can be greatly enhanced by having a mentor, who gives clear, loving guidance.

ONE WORD
1998

April 1998 in Oregon. We had been working on the remodel of the bed and breakfast for eight months. When the house was torn out to the studs, roof removed, everything went wrong. The contractor, who I mistakenly thought was trustworthy, had to be replaced. My romantic relationship ended, and I needed a job to finance the completion of the remodel. I moved into the two-room cottage next to the house and worried. I felt at rock bottom and fearful, crying in between looking at web sites and newspapers for job openings.

My work experience was in project management. Those jobs were only in large cities and hard to come by. I was a long way from a large city.

In May, my friend Denise, in Seattle, called to see how my project was going. When she understood what shape I was in, she said, "Al and I want to give you the gift of seeing Gemma." She went on to explain that Gemma was a counselor who had helped them. After arriving in Seattle by train, I drove to Gemma's home. When the front door opened, there stood a beaming, lovely woman dressed in pink and green who gave me a hug. She seemed to exude love and light.

We sat in her living room decorated in soothing turquoise colors and paint-ings of Northwest forested mountains and ocean sunsets. She asked me what was happening. I started to cry and told my woeful tale. She waited until I was finished, then said, "I have only one word for you: surrender." When she said that, everything inside me fell into place. There was such a feeling of relief. We talked about my gut wrenching sadness and fear. It was time to allow acceptance, create a quiet space in me, and trust that my needs would be met.

When I got back to my little cottage in Oregon, I received a call the very next day from Barbara, a headhunter, I knew four years ago from Denver. I was amazed that she'd been able to track me down. She asked how I was and I said, "Barbara, I'm in a jam and desperately need a good job." She said the job market had dropped dramatically, but she would try to help me.

Three months went by without any luck. It was depressing to look out the cottage window at the skeleton of the house, knowing the winter rains would soon come, and there was no roof! Then, in August, Barbara called to say she remembered a friend in Houston, whose small company needed my expertise. She sent my resume immediately and within forty minutes a call came from Paula in Texas. She interviewed me on the phone, and along with all the data she wanted to know, I told a story of the red nose I used for stress management in my last position. She laughed her wonderful laugh. It was a brief conversation. She said I would be getting a call shortly and we hung up.

Within the next twenty minutes, the phone rang again and a man said, "I want to hear about this red nose." I was invited to Houston and accepted his job offer the night I arrived. As serendipity would have it, I had a dear friend in Oregon, who was a homebuilder. She was in between jobs, so I hired her to oversee the completion of the bed and breakfast while I worked in Houston. By the time the work in Texas was done a year and a half later, the bed and breakfast was completed.

From "Surrender" to all my financial needs being met was only 90 days!

🗝 **Breathe, surrender, be calm and trust that all is in divine order.**

SWEET SISTER
2010

Crystal, who works in our office, is just the nicest woman. She always arrives at work with a cheerful smile. She's the boss's administrative assistant, has worked for the college for many years and is planning on retiring soon. There are seven of us in a room with windows on one wall giving each of us a view from our cubicles.

In her kind way, Crystal is always thinking of others, remembering everyone's birthday, being helpful to anyone within earshot, and is funny. She sings in two choirs, loves her parents, husband, children and grandchildren. And to top it all off, with her blonde hair, blue eyes, trim figure and lovely wardrobe, she's beautiful.

I was walking back to my desk one day when she introduced me to her sister, Terry. We shook hands and I said to Terry, "Did you have to bargain with God to get such a wonderful sister?" We laughed.

Crystal said she was the oldest of six children in the family. She and Terry both said they were normal sisters who were not always perfect. You could tell by the look in their eyes that they were close.

A little bit later, another co-worker, Barbara, was sitting nearby and said to me, "That was a kind way to say such a nice thing about Crystal. Where did you hear that?"

I told her, "I have never heard it before. It just came to me." In truth, I've always believed that kind words come from Love.

🗝 **There is a Loving Power that speaks through us when we allow it.**

DECEIT

1989

My friends, Harry and Kathleen were with me and my second husband, Rob, at our cabin in New Mexico. It was located on forty beautiful acres next to the national forest, alive with elk, black bear, wild turkeys, and deer.

During the visit, Rob and I had had a disagreement in private and I was upset. I stepped outside to get myself together and Kathleen joined me for a walk. She knew that our relationship was not going well.

Rob and I had had a whirlwind romance and married after knowing each other only six months. In less than a year

I learned that he and I had different ethics about money. He had hidden this information from me until just recently. What he was doing was not anything I wanted to be associated with. He was not willing to change.

As we walked, I shared with my dear friend how difficult it was to deal with the situation. She then asked me the surprising question, "Do you think he is the best the Universe has to offer you?"

Taken back I said, "I haven't thought of that!" Upon contemplation I realized, yes, there were other opportunities in this life.

Later, it paid off for me to become more aware of that potential. I discovered there were more options than I had ever allowed myself to consider.

We can give ourselves permission to have anything our heart desires, providing it does not harm us or others. Freedom begins there.

WISHES IN
THE SAND

2002

My sister, Janice, was feeling down. She looked so gloomy, and I wanted to cheer her up. I had the day off from the responsibilities at my Bed & Breakfast on the Oregon coast and devised a plan for the two of us.

She smiled when I said, "Let's go for a ride."

We drove up along the Oregon coast, enjoying the views of dark green trees above the beach framing the expanse of ocean. With the windows down, we could feel and smell the cool, moist salt sea air. We talked about everything in our lives, as if we'd left behind all troublesome reality.

Both of us were single and hoping for new love.

We stopped at a Japanese restaurant for dinner and ordered. "This will be a new experience." Janice said, as she looked down at the plate of noodles, tempura, wasabi and sushi. It was delicious.

Then we headed home, back down the coast highway, and I was pleased that my sister seemed more light hearted. We joked about how to attract the perfect man.

I spotted a pristine stretch of beach up ahead. Not a soul around. I parked the car and we walked down to the soft white sand along the water.

"I know, let's each write a description of our ideal guy in the sand! I was once told that writing our wishes down can help make them happen. We don't need to know the how or when, just what we want."

So, in the fading sunset, we each wrote a description in the sand of our idyllic partner in big letters using pieces of driftwood.

Then we held hands, turned toward the water and sent a prayer out over the waves that our dreams would come true. As we walked across the beach to the car, we started singing the old hymn we'd heard in church as children: "Praise God From Whom All Blessings Flow." We were astounded that both of us remembered the words.

Of course this story has a happy ending. The gods were with us that evening. Janice met and married her cowboy, Jay, who loved to dance and always wore his Stetson. At almost the same time, I fell for Ray, a forester, who loved to camp and fish.

Keep asking the Universe for what you really want and it could come to pass.

PERSONAL GROWTH

CABIN FEVER

1975

When we moved to Arizona, my husband and I chose to live on less so I could be home with our kids. I did the chores of cleaning, cooking, laundry, yardwork and childcare. This was meant to be the ideal life—loving husband and provider, beautiful children and a home. I'd be the mother I'd always dreamed of being, except wasn't I supposed to feel cheerful? What was this crying about?

One afternoon, frantic with worry, I decided to call my mother. I had to wait until she got home from the college where she'd started taking classes, so I waited until I saw her car in the driveway down the block.

It was a long wait at the window as I thought about my possible mental illness. As she opened her door, I dialed her number.

"Mom, there's something really wrong. I have tears on my face, but don't realize I am crying. What's happening?" She laughed. I couldn't believe she'd laugh at my distress. "I don't think this is very funny," I said, feeling hurt.

"Oh honey, you just have cabin fever. How long did you think you could sit on those brains of yours?"

"What?" She wasn't making sense.

"I want you to get a sitter tomorrow so I can take you out to the college. You'll visit my class that introduces women to education who've been away from school for a time."

She wanted to take me to Mesa Community College? I hung up the phone, not really understanding what I'd heard. But the idea of getting out of the house the next day and visiting a college class was exciting. "I can do that," I told myself.

It was all so easy. The neighbor sat with the kids. That day with Mom was fun. It was as if I'd walked out of a closed box into the sunlight. I joined the class and looked forward to every session. My weeping stopped. The cabin fever was cured.

That first class changed my life. From there I moved through other classes including a two year program in counseling. The material I studied and the teachers I had awakened a side of me I didn't know existed. God bless the wisdom of mothers.

Tears might mean a new beginning.

ACCORDING
TO WHOM?
1975

I was so excited to be back in classes. Fortunately, I was able to go during the day because there was free child care.

The Women's Movement had just gotten under way and as a married mother of three and full-time homemaker, I wasn't aware of some of that new philosophy. They were burning bras and pretty much raising the roof about women's issues. The Women and Society class sounded very intriguing and I signed up for it.

In the first class Professor Maughn began by telling us her ground rules for conducting the class. The most memorable one for me was the following:

"When you are speaking, if I hear you say the word *should*, I will interrupt you and ask, "*Should*-oughta-gotta-must, according to whom?" The purpose of asking this question is to help you understand how often you may, unconsciously, judge others with the use of that word."

I felt quite smug and certain that I was aware enough to avoid that term. Boy, was I wrong! She called me out several times which left the word *should* embedded in the back of my brain. Professor Maughn's example has helped me be less judgmental of myself and others ever since. Now, forty plus years later, I relay that same concept to the students in the Wise Women Gathering classes I teach.

Who are we to tell others how they *should* live their lives?

LAZY AND IMPATIENT

1980

When my mom was diagnosed with ovarian cancer, she began seeing a counselor, Judy, who specialized in working with cancer patients. I went to see Judy with Mom in the latter part of her illness. We met in her small pristine office with one window looking out at the city street. Judy was a petite woman with short light brown hair, didn't wear makeup and was very kind. Mom had been losing weight, had lost her hair so she wore her brown wig, which she hated, and was getting weaker. During the time with Judy, my mother felt nurtured and we were both learning about what it's like to go through a terminal illness.

After mom passed on, I continued counseling with Judy working through my grief. I came to realize the work I needed to do next was with my father, who was still alive. Going through that process healed and enhanced our relationship. I discovered that dad had not realized the part he played in making our relationship difficult. We worked through that and became much closer.

When my marriage wasn't working, counselors, Charlie and Jerry, helped me progress through divorce while taking good care of myself. Over the years, it's been life changing to be in therapy. I learned how to understand situations more clearly or how I was getting in my own way along with new and better ways to handle all kinds of challenges.

One day my son, Adam, was annoyed with my suggestion that a friend of his might benefit from seeking help. Adam had had a counseling experience that was not positive. He asked somewhat sarcastically, "How come you are so stuck on seeing counselors?"

The answer that came immediately was, "Because I'm lazy and impatient. I believe there's a reason for everything. If I am in a situation that goes badly, I want to understand it. I could spend a lot of time doing amateur research on my own, but I haven't been that ambitious or patient." I want the answer ASAP!

🔑 **The experience of counseling may make the difference between living in confusion and living an awakened life.**

HOW TO MEASURE HAPPINESS

1985

I was exhausted after work. When I got home, I fixed dinner, talked over the day with my three kids while we ate and, later, got them to bed. Then I faced the phone ringing into the evening from friends who wanted me to listen to their personal dramas. Something had to go and it couldn't be the kids or the job.

I thought about my friends' problems and noticed a theme in most of them. They often had a repetitious negative situation they wanted me to fix. It was nice for me to feel needed, but I noticed that they seldom asked me how my life was going. Even when I offered my ideas about what might help, they seldom followed through. Two weeks later I'd hear the same story, with no solution.

Contemplating an answer to this predicament, I was reminded of my long ago friend and mentor, Jerry Brown. I met him when I was twenty one at a sales meeting in my parents' living room. He gave a compelling presentation. A dynamic salesman, he dressed like a professional businessman in a nice-looking leather jacket. He stood tall and handsome with a military flat-top haircut, and a warm, inspiring speaking voice.

A surprising part of Jerry's life, I later learned, was his spiritual path. Over the next couple of years, he introduced my mother and me to the world of metaphysics, the study of spirituality.

One of the many teachings he shared began with the question, "How do you measure happiness?" Responding to my questioning look, he explained, "One of the ways to know how happy you are is to take an inventory of the energy you keep around you, the energy of the people in your life."

I asked, "How do I do that?"

Jerry said, "Make a list of the people you have invited into your life and how much positive or negative energy they each bring. That might give you some perspective about your choices up until now."

When I took a current inventory of my friends, co-workers and acquaintances, I could see the pattern. Feeling needed was not making me happy any longer. I felt a hunger for the company of people who had an uplifting and optimistic outlook on life. It was time to ease out of the old relationships that were negative, so I became less available. Now my goal was to spend more time with nurturing, interesting and healthy people. I took some college classes and got more involved in spiritual studies which helped me achieve that goal; giving me a broader, happier point of view.

🗝 **When I surrounded myself with positive energy it led to more peace, wisdom and joy.**

TRUST YOUR DREAMS
1985

On my way to my son's football game one afternoon, I saw a billboard advertising new homes that looked intriguing and very reasonably priced. It caught my attention because I'd been thinking about moving to a nicer place. After the game I went back to the subdivision, checked out the models and found one that was just what I'd been dreaming of.

In the sales office, I chose a lot in the subdivision—but it had already been sold. Actually, as a thirty five year old single mom I wouldn't qualify for the home at that time anyway, due to my low paying job as a warehouse manager. But I didn't forget that house.

A year later, I was asked by my boss to assist another company that was opening a new business in our area. They needed my help because I was the only one who had contact with the type of technicians they needed to hire. During our lunch, while discussing their budget for personnel, I realized I wanted the management position they would be offering.

I got up the nerve to say, "For a manager, I think you need someone who has experience in this business and knows the local talent. I believe I'm just that person." I looked around the table. "Of course you'd need to raise the salary for a manager with those qualifications." I added with a smile. We all laughed. They asked a few more questions, and the meeting ended.

I went back to my job, feeling discouraged. I could tell that the idea of hiring a woman in that position was received as a joke. Generally, only men were hired in management positions on the technical side of the business back in the 80s. Then I remembered my philosophy, the "rules" defined by others about what is possible do not apply to me. I waited.

Two months later, on Christmas Eve, I was in the office parking lot sitting in my company car when the two gentlemen I'd had lunch with called and offered me the job at the higher salary I'd suggested. My heart pounded, and I thought, *"I think I have a negotiating advantage."* So I got up the courage to also ask for a company truck and three weeks paid vacation. They groaned and agreed to the deal. It was the biggest raise I'd ever had! I was so excited!

I went house shopping the next weekend. When I found a house I wanted, I was told they couldn't put it on the lot I preferred. Rather than give up, I remembered the house from the year before that I'd liked. I drove back over to that subdivision. To my delight and astonishment, the lot that had been previously sold was now available—and the model that I loved was reduced in price. It seemed that waiting for what I wanted had served me well. I bought that house!!

🔑 **Realizing your dreams may require patience, belief in yourself and plenty of courage.**

WATCH THE BIRDS

1993

I was in counseling, once again contemplating why another relationship had failed. I wanted to get the sadness over quickly, understand what had happened and avoid repeating old mistakes.

I had heard that Bob was a gifted counselor. When I arrived at his office I felt anxious, but comfortable in the black leather chair he offered me. He was a soft spoken man with dark hair and blue eyes. He wore a beige V-neck sweater over a light blue button-down collared shirt and jeans. He sat across from me at a tidy oak desk and asked me what had been happening in my life. For the next three visits, we discussed my relationship history. By the fourth visit I asked what his insights were.

He said, "Here is my observation. You are an intelligent, attractive, ambitious woman. You are a loving and committed mom. You have good business sense and good judgment, which is reflected in your successful career." He paused while I tried to take that in.

"In choosing a love in your life," he added, "you will need to find that rare man who is comfortable with those qualities in a woman, and doesn't feel a need to compete with you."

"How do I do that?" I wondered, and felt the tears well up. I blew my nose, knowing Bob's counsel was true.

My counselor looked deeply into my eyes and I felt the strength he gave me. Before I left he said one more thing, and I've never forgotten the image. "Have you ever noticed how birds fly? They fly in close formation, but they fly independently. One cannot fly for another."

🗝 **Find the mate who is comfortable in their own skin.**

IMAGES OF CALM
1994

It was 1994 in the summer heat of Arizona. I was working with a boss who was a bully. He harassed his administrative assistant and verbally abused the other women in the office, including me. My job had become so upsetting that I wasn't sleeping, felt paranoid, and was so intimidated that I couldn't answer his questions correctly. I felt a 'deer in the headlights' panicky feeling, couldn't think clearly. After walking away from him, I knew the answers and knew he was a bully, but I felt trapped by his attacks.

I decided to see my counselor, Jack. He was a nice looking, laid back, tall man with blonde hair and brown eyes. He knew me as a competent, intelligent and successful manager. When I explained what was going on at work, he mentioned using "the easy fix". He asked me to sit back on the comfy couch in his office, close my eyes, take a few deep breaths and imagine a beautiful place where I felt calm and safe. I chose a sunny day in the forest looking up at fluffy white clouds in a blue sky. I was lying on a huge, warm flat rock with my hand extended into a little waterfall next to me, the water trickling through my fingers. The sun was warm and the water was cool.

Then he said, "Hold that picture for a moment. Now, visualize a TV screen showing your boss's head and shoulders in the upper half of it. Now take the picture from the forest and make it a small picture down in the lower right hand part of the screen."

He snapped his fingers five times. "Now I want you to grow the small picture large enough to completely cover your boss's image." Then he snapped his fingers again.

He said, "The next time you get that 'deer in the headlights' panicky feeling you need to envision that same scene in the woods—like a movie—over taking whatever the situation is with your boss."

"Can I do that? Won't people think I'm crazy?" I asked.

"No one will know what you're doing. You'll be able to pay attention to the conversation and won't have the fear again." Jack sounded certain and I believed him.

The process worked the very first time I tried it!

My boss couldn't believe how calm and confident I was. He couldn't intimidate me. I saw it in his face—baffled, surprised. That process has worked ever since.

🔑 **A peaceful and serene demeanor can be very powerful.**

MUD ON
THE CARPET

1995

Dan came in the house from the muddy back yard, did not take his filthy boots off and proceeded to walk through the kitchen, dining room, living room and to the bathroom on the new beige carpet! I felt instantly so angry I wanted to yell, *"What are you doing? How unbelievably inconsiderate of you!!"* I was red with rage inside and just wanted to lose it!

Then I thought, "Wait a minute. I don't normally get this angry. This level of outrage is way beyond just mud on the carpet. What else is going on?" Thank goodness I caught myself before saying things I would regret.

Thinking about it the rest of the day did not give me any answers, so I called our counselor, Neil, for an appointment. We had seen him as a couple a few times recently and he had complimented us on how well our relationship was going.

Upon arriving at Neil's pleasant, carpeted, cool office I explained the story and expressed how mystified I was by what I perceived as an overreaction.

Neil said, "I know you well enough to know that you are very sensitive. You prefer soft colors and fabrics in your clothing and in your home. Beauty is very important to you. Would you say that's true?"

"Yes, it is."

He sat back in his office chair, paused a moment and said, "Is it possible that your lovely home is like part of your skin and when someone tromps on it with muddy boots, they are tromping on you?"

That explained it!

That night at dinner, Dan and I talked about how upset I had been earlier. I explained, "I learned how important it is to me to keep the house clean and attractive.

Would you please help in doing that?" He kissed me and said "Yes, of course, and I'm sorry about the boots." All was well.

🔑 **Our surroundings may be more important than we realize.**

IN THE NEXT
TEN MINUTES

1994

Nikki was sent to me by a friend. We sat on my comfortable couch with a cup of hot tea. I asked her, "What brings you here?"

She started talking very fast, "My life is out of control and falling apart both personally and professionally. I own a publishing company which is having financial problems. I have gone through two relationships in the past year and a half. I am having migraine headaches and I don't sleep well." And there was more. I quietly listened until she finished.

Then I asked, "What do you want to do next to take gentle good care of yourself?"

She said," I don't know."

"I think you do, and it's important for you to know, not me."

"I'll think about that and get back to you." I smiled to myself, having been in the same place myself in the past.

Several days later Nikki called and said, with excitement, "I figured out the answer to your question. I just signed up with a health club and will be going three days a week."

"I think that's great and when I asked you that question, I meant *in the next ten minutes.*"

"I don't understand. What do you mean?"

"Taking gentle good care of yourself may be as simple as a deep breath, stretch and a roll of your shoulders. Take a drink of water, walk outside, or simply have a quiet moment to slow down."

Three weeks later, Nikki called to tell me she had been practicing what we talked about and life seemed so much more effortless and peaceful.

🔑 **Caring for ourselves first gives us the energy to care for everything else.**

WEE ONE WITHIN

1995

During a meditation session, our wise leader asked us to close our eyes and visualize ourselves at the youngest age we could remember. The room was dim and quiet. My first image was me about the age of six with a big smile on my face sitting on a tricycle. I was wearing a red plaid dress, had long wavy red hair, freckles, and a broken right arm in a cast and sling.

When we had the image in our minds, we were instructed to put that image into a TV screen. Then imagine walking into that screen, looking down at the child and scolding her with the names we'd call ourselves when we did something stupid.

I heard others' muffled weeping nearby. Unable to imagine saying those things, I stood by the child and didn't say anything.

I waited. The next direction was to bend down and hold that youngster in my arms, tell her how much I loved her and how special she was. That was easy. She was so adorable.

After a few moments, we were told to end the visualization. I was so moved by that experience that I went home and found one of those small black and white school pictures of myself in the first grade. I put it on my refrigerator where I would see it often. I wanted to remind myself of who I was taking care of, that little me inside.

Years later, I was clearing the breakfast table and I dropped my knife covered with raspberry jam and it left a red stripe on my clean white shirt. After wiping the jam off, I went outside to the heat of the Arizona morning to plant some flowers. I managed to spill potting soil on the grass making a big black mess. I began to clean that up and wondered what might happen next.

About half way through planting, I was thirsty so I went into the house, fixed a tall glass of iced tea, brought it outside and put it down near me. Moving the hose to water the flowers, I knocked over my glass and there went my fresh cold drink! I started to scold myself, but then remembered the little girl on the bike with her sweet smile and broken arm inside me and knew I couldn't chastise her. I was a grown woman now, an adult with a few klutzy moments. Not a big deal. I took a deep breath and thought with a smile, "Welcome to being a human being."

🔑 **Kindness given to our Inner Child allows us to accept ourselves the rest of our lives.**

TAKE YOUR HAND
OFF THE BURNER

1997

We had moved to Oregon to begin remodeling the bed and breakfast. My partner, Dan, tall, blond and blue eyed, a talented landscaper, was excited about the plan. At first, we both had the same ideas about how we wanted to design and remodel the house. As the project progressed, things became more contentious between us.

One evening we invited friends and family over to our apartment for dinner. Dan was preparing a delicious menu of sweet onion soup, fresh caught wild salmon, red potatoes, mixed vegetables, and a fresh fruit tart for dessert. I was the chef's helper, except I wasn't pleasing the chef.

"Don't put that dish over there," he said, ordering me around. "Keep out of the way! Help me over here."

I felt hurt and embarrassed by his behavior, but I kept a cheerful attitude, thinking he was just stressed.

At dinner, Dan didn't stop. He made fun of my attempt to make a special dish for him the day before. He mocked the sweater I was wearing. Feeling humiliated and angry, I ignored his comments with a fake smile.

During the meal my sister looked at me, waiting for me to defend myself. She cornered me as we were clearing the dishes and asked, "Why do you put up with that? It's not like you. You wouldn't allow anyone else to say those things to you."

I had no response, and turned away with tears in my eyes. It occurred to me that I'd been making excuses for Dan's unkindness for several weeks.

Then I remembered my friend and counselor, Joyce, saying, "Take your hand off the burner." She taught me, a long time ago, that pain is a wake-up call.

She believed that emotional pain unaddressed caused what she called "dis-ease", meaning disease. I was asking for illness if I kept ignoring the pain I was in.

The next day I went to Dan and said, "I'm not going to put up with such bitter unkindness in the way you speak to me any longer."

"I'm sorry. I'm pretty sure it's due to my depression," he said.

"Then you need to get help."

"I've tried medication and it doesn't work. And I'm not going to counseling. Let's just start over, and it'll be fine."

I knew why his medication didn't work; he didn't take it regularly.

Things between us improved for a short time, but soon the verbal abuse returned. I wasn't going to smile and ignore it any more. I asked him to leave, and he did. My pain went out the door with him.

Removing pain from our lives is freeing, nurturing and healthy.

MEMORY
REPLACEMENT
1998

San Diego was once my favorite place in the whole world. Living there was delightful. I loved being close to the ocean, had a dream job, lived in a charming blue cottage with white trim, and enjoyed the people I met there.

Two years later serious problems became apparent at work. I filed a lawsuit. The experience became so stressful that I no longer enjoyed the glories of the coastal beauty, gentle weather and captivating places to visit. When I returned to Arizona and family, I left behind bitter memories.

Because I had had a painful experience in the workplace, my recollections about life in San Diego were tainted with grief and sorrow. The job ended there and I had been treated badly.

So it was time to return.

I needed to remember all that I had enjoyed about that lovely place and let the sad memories evaporate, replaced by new experiences.

As soon as I got to San Diego, I walked on the beach, watching the blue green waves with their awesome, thundering sound, feeling the warm sand on my feet, breathing in the salt sea air and remembered the good times.

My favorite Mexican restaurant that served wonderful shrimp tacos was still there. I ordered a plateful to remind me how much I enjoyed the taste of San Diego. Eating delicious tacos on the beach was the perfect medicine.

The cottage where I had lived looked the same. The brilliant blue morning glories we had planted in the yard were thriving, and they looked gorgeous.

The wide open sunset view of the ocean from the front of the little house was still breathtaking. I remembered the people who visited us and the good times we'd shared as if I'd stepped into a movie featuring me and my friends.

It was uplifting to recapture the peace, joy and beauty of the enchanting place I'd known in the past.

The wounds were now healed.

🔑 **Consciously replacing hurtful memories with new ones may give us back our wholeness.**

RED LIGHT
2000

I had chosen to have my breast cancer surgery in Phoenix to be near my family in case it did not go well. My days at work in Houston leading up to the surgery seemed to go slowly, and, of course, I was anxious.

I didn't want to worry the family with my fears, so I called my mentor and dear friend, Sherry, who was the one person I could be open with before I headed to Phoenix. Talking with Sherry always helped me through crises.

She answered the phone with, "What's the matter?" Her instincts were always keen, and she knew me well.

I started to cry and blurted out, "Sherry, I'm only fifty two and I have breast cancer! I'm scared. My mom and grandmother died at a young age from ovarian cancer. I had a hysterectomy and thought I was safe from this terrible disease. It doesn't look it right now."

"Do you understand that this is a red light, not a yellow light?" she asked. It was the most meaningful message given to me through the whole experience.

I knew instantly what she meant. It was time to stop, to observe and evaluate, take a long look. My life at that time was chaotic with many challenges. I had been working for eighteen months in Houston, living in a hotel trying to make enough money to finish remodeling a bed and breakfast in Oregon. At the same time, I was going through a lawsuit in San Diego! I thought I could manage, do it all, if I could just have one more year of that big fat income.

Then reality struck. I remember sitting at my desk in Houston when the phone rang. It was a nurse in Phoenix at my doctor's office telling me that my recent mammogram did not look good.

They were sending it FedEx to arrive in the morning. They wanted me to see an oncologist in the next forty-eight hours. I instantly felt cold and numb. Luckily, I worked with a woman who had had nose cancer, a double mastectomy, and had survived. We were friends and she got me to her oncologist the next day. It was confirmed to be breast cancer.

Cancer was my red light. I needed to change my life completely and immediately. There was no doubt that I had overburdened myself, thinking I was indestructible. My body had had enough and proved me wrong.

I am now a twenty year breast cancer survivor. I live a quiet life as a teacher, author and life coach, which I love. Better choices made a better life. God bless Sherry for her guidance.

If I push myself too far, my body will stop me.

HAPPY VALENTINE'S DAY TO ME

2000

I had scheduled Valentine's Day for the second breast cancer surgery because it seemed like it would bring good luck. The previous surgeon had missed some of the cancer the first time.

My friend, Sandi, invited me to stay with her while I had my operation. She lived a few miles from the Mayo Clinic and took me there, staying with me for moral support. The first procedure was to inject nuclear dye into the tumor site. The dye would allow the surgeon to see the exact location of the tumor so they could be certain any remnant of it would be removed and see if any lymph nodes contained cancer.

After those preliminaries, surgery was scheduled for three hours later at the hospital. I asked the radiation tech if we could go to Sandi's house nearby to pass the time.

"Sure, just don't bump the area of the dye needle," he said. The needle site was covered with a Styrofoam cup and taped to my chest.

At Sandi's house I read my email and had some tea, relaxing a little. We got back to the hospital ten minutes early.

A nurse took me back to the surgery prep area behind hanging curtains where I put on my hospital gown and got into the bed. All of a sudden the curtain was snatched back and there stood my surgeon, saying in a furious voice, "Where have you been?"

"I had permission to go home with my friend for the three-hour wait," I said, trembling at the sight of my very angry doctor.

"Who gave you permission?" she demanded.

"I don't know," I said, "a radiation tech, I think."

She snapped, "We've been looking for you! There was a cancellation and we wanted to do your surgery earlier than scheduled, but we couldn't find you." Then she turned on her heel and stomped to a nearby phone. I heard her say, "Who gave my patient permission to go home rather than directly to the hospital?" After she got an answer, she slammed the phone down.

Oh no! The doctor who's really mad at me is about to cut me open! My eyes started to fill with tears. The nurse standing next to me said, "Don't worry. It's not your fault."

I didn't want to go into surgery feeling fearful and upset. Then I had an idea!

I asked for the patient satisfaction survey form, and the nurse handed it to me with a smile. I could tell that not everyone was happy working with this doctor. I filled out the form, telling the truth about what happened and how unhappy I was about it. The nurse promised to get it back to the right people. Then I asked her, "Would someone go to the waiting room and bring my friend, Sandi, in to be with me?" She happily responded, "Of course."

When Sandi got to my bedside, I asked her for my purse, rummaged around in it for my red clown nose that I always carried with me. I put it on. Those around me laughed and I felt much better. Just then the curtain opened again. It was the anesthesiologist who immediately pointed at the red nose and said, "Oooh, I like that! You have to wear that into surgery!" When I agreed, he left with a grin on his face.

As I waited, with the curtain partly open, there seemed to be a parade of hospital personnel coming by for a peek—and smiling. As they wheeled me to the surgery forty-five minutes later, I saw my surgeon talking on a desk phone. When she saw me with my red nose on her mouth dropped open. I smiled and waved to her.

The red nose stayed on while they put me to sleep. I felt calm and happy. That nose is still in my purse twenty years later and comes in handy for road rage and crying babies.

Happy Valentine's Day!

In the midst of a frightening experience, it is possible to regain a sense of empowerment and find a way to smile.

SUPERWOMAN
TO THE RESCUE

2007

The doctor said to my father, "I'm sorry to tell you that the news is not good. The red spot below your lower lip is merkle cell skin cancer, a rare fast moving cancer more serious than melanoma. I have only seen seven in my fifteen years of practice. Another disturbing factor is the Gleason score, which measures the aggressiveness of the cell. Your score is an eight, ten being terminal."

We sat across from this kind doctor in shocked silence. I'd come to the hospital with Dad, as I always did, to find out the results of his biopsy. We weren't expecting such bad news—worse than melanoma? Dad had been having small pre-cancerous growths taken off his head, face and neck for many years, but we'd never heard of the merkle cell.

After the doctor answered our questions, and we'd made plans for surgery, we thanked him and left. I held Dad's hand as we walked to the parking garage in silence.

I went into rescue mode. My mind rushed to arrange everything: I'd take time off work to go to his appointments and surgery, even though it was a four-hour round trip drive for me. I'd be the comforter when Dad was depressed. I'd research the type of cancer and get some other opinions. No one else in the family was as efficient and organized as I was. I was Superwoman.

As we were driving home, I explained to Dad the plans I had to help him out.

"You can't do that," he said. "You live too far away. We have family nearby who will help me."

"I'll figure out a way!" I insisted.

"No you won't. I don't want you to."

I drove on, wondering if he was right. What compelled me to take care of him from a distance when someone from the family was nearer to dad? Why would I take on this burden? Why couldn't I trust a family member to step up, let Dad make his own decisions? Where did that come from?

It came to me. I'd done it many times before—as the oldest child of five, single mom, manager of people at work, and now adult daughter—Superwoman taking over. I became a hyper alert overachiever.

I pulled into Dad's driveway. We got out of the car and walked up the porch steps. I took a deep breath, relaxed into reality, knowing someone close by was perfectly capable of helping. It was what he wanted. I brought myself back to loving daughter mode and dropped my Superwoman cape on the floor, letting it crumble into dust.

If the responsibility is not mine then I can let go, knowing I am always enough.

SERIOUSLY?

2005

Jennifer was telling me about a fabulous all-expense paid business trip she and her husband were taking to Greece. She said they had saved some money for travel on their own, as well, and were so excited. How wonderful was that, to be able to travel, have it be paid for and have extra money for shopping and side trips? Then I heard her say that she was so stressed over what clothes to buy to take on the trip. She said the dilemma was ruining all the fun of planning.

I rolled my eyes when I looked at her and said, "I'd feel for you, but I can't reach you."

I meant, "You have to be kidding me! When you focus on the matters of wardrobe, it spoils the joy of planning a fantastic experience? "Oh, brother!"

She grinned and gave me a hug.

Humor, when we hear whining, may remind us to be grateful.

WORK / CAREER

WILLINGNESS
TO WORK
1967

I've had an interesting working life—from waitress to executive. I graduated from high school at age seventeen, had one year of college, and the next year was married. Nine months later my husband received his draft letter and joined the Air Force. In our time in the service we travelled from to Biloxi, Mississippi, to England, and back home to Michigan for me, while he served in the Phillippines.supporting the troops in Vietnam.

Looking back, I can see how resourceful I was as a young woman. I was happy to supplement our income during those early years, as a waitress in a Walgreen's restaurant, a typist and accounting clerk, and a temp for Kelly Services working several different administrative jobs.

When my husband came back home from overseas, he left the Air Force and we moved from Michigan to Arizona. By 1973 we had three children and were living on one income. Money was tight.

I figured I could save some money if I had a sewing machine and could make some of the kids' clothes, but I needed an extra $100.00 to buy the machine. Then, within a week, the opportunity came to work for my dad's insurance man, making appointments. I jumped at the chance. It was telephone work I could do from home.

The pay was twenty-five cents for every insurance policy renewal date I could get, and fifty cents for an appointment to see the agent. I paid for that sewing machine in six weeks! Later, I sold Sarah Coventry jewelry at home-parties in the evening when my husband was home from work.

After earning a two-year counseling certificate at the community college, my marriage ended suddenly. Divorce can be very motivating. After six years of hard work at several low paying jobs, I began a career in a corporate environment and was able to move up the ladder to several successful jobs in management, allowing me to buy a new home. After the children were grown, a dream job opened up in California and I took it.

In all those married years I found ways to help supplement my husband's income, and, as a single mom, I took any job I could do to take care of my family. I always remembered that if times got tough, I could still waitress, type, file, answer the phone, sell jewelry or take care of children.

If I was willing to do whatever it took, with my hands as well as my head, there were more opportunities to be successful.

ANGER WITH HUMOR

1985

The truck driver was fuming when he came into our office. He was livid about the service he had received from one of our technicians. He didn't find out that the repair on his phone had not worked until he got out on the road.

I came out to greet him by asking, "How are you today?"

"I'm fine," he growled, his face furious.

"How come your eyes and mouth don't match?" That was true. He had huge blue eyes that were scrunched into an awful frown. They shot daggers at me.

He broke up laughing at my question, caught in my web. His body relaxed and those eyes looked at me pleasantly. He handed me his phone, and I smiled at him, ready to solve the problem.

The next day I met with Chuck, a frustrated manager ready to shout his complaints. "*This is not my week*," I thought.

I had travelled to Omaha to help him with a remodel of his store which would better accommodate his growing business.

Chuck greeted me just inside the door and began reeling off everything that had been going wrong. He had barely let me inside and was standing very close to my face.

I listened to his outburst for a minute then reached over and touched his arm saying slowly. "Chuck, I can't tell if you're breathing, which is making me nervous. I could pay better attention if I knew you were breathing."

It stopped him and he took a deep breath. We both laughed.

Then we moved into his office and talked in a more relaxed—and productive—manner.

I have to admit that I treated Chuck with my secret weapon. It works when you ask someone who's upset if they are breathing. They usually laugh, and that's the secret.

I could have tried it with the trucker, but I got him to laugh anyway.

🔑 **Humor can help establish compassion and open a space for a more constructive conversation.**

JOYFUL TERMINATION

1988

Sharon's performance at our company was not going well. She didn't get along with her co-workers in customer service and was rude to customers. I'd given her several warnings that she had ignored. It was my job to let her go, and it wasn't what I really wanted to do because she had good administrative talents and worked hard. But she had poor communication skills.

When she came into my office that afternoon, she seemed pleased to see me but kind of down. I liked her, and she knew it. She was just twenty three, and she had potential if we could tap into it.

"Why are you so unhappy here?" I began, catching her off guard.

She tried to smile. "I don't know," she replied, avoiding an answer that might get her in trouble.

"Why did you choose to work here?" I persisted.

"I needed the money. Saw it in the paper." She was twisting her hands in her lap, shredding a tissue in the process.

"So what's wrong with customer service?"

"Lots of things," she began, sounding defensive. "People are rude and impatient. I get so frustrated!" More hand twisting.

"Well, what activities make you happy?"

"I like artwork and fashion," she said, looking more alive now.

"Have you ever thought about graphic arts or fashion design as a career?"

She leaned forward and said, "Oh, what a dream, to be able to do something like that!"

"If I could get you an appointment with someone in that line of work, would you be interested?"

"Oh, that would be fabulous!" she said, dropping the tissue.

"Well, maybe we could work on a change together."

Sharon jumped from her chair and hugged me.

Within a week we found her an entry level position in graphic design in our technical division.

For the first time in my career, I learned that firing someone could be a happy experience!

🗝 **Asking questions rather than making statements, invites people to partner in solving problems.**

TAR BABY

1987

After Phil's meeting with the boss, he walked up to my desk and angrily accused me of not supporting him. I had no clue what he was talking about. What did he want from me? We hadn't worked closely together, but he seemed to be in trouble and wanted me to be a part of it.

I'd been in a good mood, going about my business, working on the project, and we were making headway. Evidently Phil wasn't. I had no way of knowing his problem because he just stood there, red in the face and furious.

He was middle aged, bald and a little overweight. "Couldn't you see I needed back-up? Aren't you aware we're running out of time? Why couldn't you offer more staff?" he bellowed.

None of that made any sense. What did he mean? If I could be drawn into Phil's troubles, he could blame me? I considered his reasons for coming to me and tried to imagine what he needed. It was evident that Phil needed support from me without troubling to ask nicely or explain what the problem was. He had expected me to guess his predicament. Was I supposed to be a part of a drama I knew nothing about?

Then I remembered the Tar Baby story. Brer Bear is determined to trap Brer Rabbit by putting a ball of tar with a face on it on a stump near Brer Rabbit's path. Brer Rabbit walks down the path in the forest and goes by the smiling Tar Baby sitting on the stump. As he walks by, Brer Rabbit says, "Good mawnin!" Tar Baby just sits there silently smiling. Brer Rabbit stops. Then he walks back to Tar Baby and says, "I said, Good mawnin!" Nothing. Brer Rabbit gets upset and hollers again.

There's still no answer from that smiling Tar Baby. Brer Rabbit gets so angry that he hauls off and slugs the Tar Baby in the chest, and his hand gets stuck in the tar. "Let me go!" says Brer Rabbit. When he can't get his first hand out, he hits Tar Baby with his other hand which gets stuck in the tar. The next thing you know, Brer Rabbit's hands and feet are all stuck in the tar. Now he's trapped.

I am smarter than Brer Rabbit. If I tried to help this angry guy, this Tar Baby, I'd get my hands and feet stuck. I wanted no part of whatever Phil's drama was about. This was not my problem, and I knew I couldn't help.

I looked up from my papers and told Phil I didn't understand anything he was talking about. Let the record say he walked away, incensed.

🗝 **Be aware of any attempt to be drawn into a situation that does not belong to you.**

LIFE CAN BE "STRETCHFUL"

1993

On my birthday I met with my friend, Carol, to discuss what my upcoming birth year had in store. Carol was a middle-aged, gray haired gal with a little extra weight on her. She had green eyes, a great smile and sense of humor. I enjoyed her insights into life. She used the word "stretchful" to describe what I could be expecting this year.

I replied that "stressful" wasn't anything new.

"No," she said. I meant "stretchful," which perplexed me. What an unusual term! She wouldn't explain further and left it to me to get a sense of what she meant.

That understanding would soon come.

A year later, when moving to a new home, I remembered that conversation and laughed. What had happened the past year was all of "stretchful". The company I worked for tried to fire me without cause. The vice president had asked me to take a position which was politically dangerous and had promised to support me if I would take the job. I accepted and over the next year developed a budget process making the regional managers accountable for questionable spending which meant taking away their individual budget control. The vice president gave me high praise for the excellent job I had done.

My changes were certainly not welcomed by those managers. "Stretchful" was taking on real meaning. Just after the new plan was implemented, I received a directive from the vice president to come to Seattle. There was going to be a meeting with all the regional managers, he said, and he wanted me to attend. The meeting time had been changed and I was not notified. Rather than meeting with the managers,

I was called into Chet's office later that afternoon. The meeting had been held without me. Chet reported to the Vice President and was known to be his hatchet man. The truth was I had been called to Seattle to be terminated, for no reason other than the regional managers were "finding me difficult to work with."

After firing me, Chet said, "You have lots of friends in the company. You'll be able to find another job." I had just received my eleventh consecutive outstanding annual performance appraisal two weeks prior. The decision made no sense. I left in shock.

After the short meeting, I went to the airport, but before getting on the plane, I had the presence of mind to call a nearby friend, Denise. She said, "Don't leave yet. Come over, stay with me and we'll talk about it."

By the time I got to her house, I knew I wasn't going to just cave in to Chet's directive. Denise agreed.

The next morning, I was at the Human Resources Department at 8:00 a.m. sharp, requesting all of the original contents of my personnel file. The staff member said they might not be able to find it for me right away. I stated, "I'm not leaving until I have that file in my hand." Of course, it was handed to me in about twenty minutes.

I left for my flight home to Phoenix after verifying the file contents were complete. At home that night, I got a call from the only female officer on the board of directors. She said, "The word about your dismissal has spread around corporate headquarters and everyone is stunned. How are you doing?"

"I'm still in shock, scared and don't know what to do." She said to me, "You need to stop being afraid right now! You are a female over forty and a protected minority. Let me give you the address of an attorney whom I worked with in Phoenix."

I called the attorney and made an appointment. He was not encouraging once he found out he would be dealing with one of the largest telecommunications companies in the country. I sensed he would not be of help, and my case seemed hopeless.

The next weekend, I was talking with a friend about what had happened and she said, "I have the name of a terrific female attorney in Phoenix." She made an appointment for me with the attorney, Laura. When I got to her small office, I discovered she was a no nonsense gal. The only picture on her office wall was an early black and white picture of John Lennon sitting on the hood of an old Ford with his guitar. I liked that.

After reviewing all of my documentation, Laura told me she believed I had an excellent case. She knew that I was concerned about legal costs, so her plan was to coach me in my written communication with the company. I would create my e-mails and documents then send them to her. She would only charge me in fifteen minutes increments for her review and approval. Then I would send them off. What a blessing!

I notified the company in writing that I was not accepting their offer of two week's severance pay and was refusing to leave. Gloria, the head of Human Resources asked me to fly to Seattle for a discussion a few weeks later. When I got to the meeting, she and Chet, the hatchet man, were sitting next to each other at a table laughing. It was obvious they were in cahoots. At one point in the conversation, I got really upset, but didn't want them to know, so I went to the bathroom, had a few tears, took some deep breaths and got the strength to go back to the meeting.

They threatened me with an expensive lawsuit and told me I didn't have a leg to stand on. Luckily, I had a plan. I offered them three choices. The company could give me the old job back, or give me a new job with no salary reduction and the same opportunity for advancement—or go to court. It was their turn to be surprised. I walked out and went back to Phoenix standing much straighter. Never mind that my stomach was flip flopping.

For the next five months I stayed home and the paychecks kept coming. There were conference calls, more e-mails and memos, none of which were responding to my offer and I reminded them of it often.

Finally, the vice president, who hired me, met me face-to-face at the home office and asked me what I thought should happen. I laid my hand on his arm and said, "I trust you implicitly." He dropped his head on the table and said, "I knew you were going to say that." We had known each other for ten years and had been friends. He knew he had betrayed me and I knew he had a conscience. Within a month, a job in Phoenix was offered and I accepted. The salary was the same, the opportunities were the same and all was made nice.

That could be considered a "stretchful" year.

Operating according to one's own principles enhances a sense of personal empowerment.

TAKE A LEAP
1995

I was at a single's party on New Year's Eve enjoying myself. Winter in Phoenix was balmy, and some of us were outside by the pool talking about our resolutions for the coming year.

If there was anything I wanted, it was to change my job. I'd hit the glass ceiling where I was working, and I'd been there for eleven years. Words came to me: "I'd like a job that utilizes all my gifts and talents, where I'm appreciated and make a difference in people's lives." Those criteria would leave me open to any industry. A new place would be an adventure.

After the New Year began, I didn't put out a resume. I was concerned that it might become known that I was looking for a different job and could be let go. Besides, I totally trusted that the Universe was powerful enough to make anything happen, and I stayed focused on that resolution.

However, by November nothing had happened, and I wondered if I had not done enough to bring on the desired outcome. I got the answer the next day. The phone rang in my cubicle as I was returning from lunch. It was a woman from an employment agency asking if I was interested in a job change.

"How did you get my name?" I asked.

"My boss will talk to you about that if you're interested."

I took a chance. This felt like an adventure already. "Okay. Let me speak to your boss, please."

The boss, Barbara, got on the line and said that my name had come up in conversations around the country regarding project management. "I am offering you the opportunity to interview in San Diego.

The expenses will be covered." She went on to describe the complex job I'd be interviewing for.

I hadn't interviewed for a job in eleven years and thought it would be good practice. I was sure I wouldn't get the job, but I went anyway. As the plane took off, I felt calm and thought of it as a fun trip.

The people in San Diego were starting a new technology in telecommunications, and they needed personnel. I noticed everyone was dressed in casual clothes and there was laughter in a very relaxed atmosphere in the large office. The woman who was interviewing me asked if I had any material related to the job I was currently doing. I showed her the single legal size spread sheet I used to manage my projects quite simply. She read it, then excused herself and returned with two gentlemen who wanted to know more about my management style. After answering their questions, I thought they would be great people to work with, but the job of managing the buildout of a large new digital network seemed out of my league. They asked me where I would want to be located, Los Angeles or San Diego? I told them San Diego seemed like a wonderful location, right by the ocean, one of my favorite places to be. We laughed, shook hands and they thanked me for coming.

I got home to Phoenix by three o'clock that afternoon. By five o'clock, I got a call from San Diego offering me the job. Taking this position sounded very daunting. Then I thought, "The worst thing that could happen would be that I would fail at the job and go find another one." I accepted.

My New Year's resolution had come true. In my new position, I had the freedom and authority to use my gifts and talents, was paid well, felt appreciated and I like to believe that I made a difference in the lives of those with whom I worked. It turned out to be the most successful position of my career.

Being afraid, willing to take a chance and saying yes can produce amazing outcomes.

PROCESS PERFECTION

1995

In the beginning we knew we had an enormously challenging project. We had accepted the deadline of completing the job of building 275 towers in two years in California. As project managers, my partner and I had a conference call with the vice president at the home office just a few months into the job. We were told our two-year timeline had been cut to an impossible eighteen months. My mouth dropped open, and we looked at each other totally stunned. We were asked, "Can you make this new deadline on time?" We said, "Yes, we'll make it work." Now the pressure was really on.

We had eight employees and five contractors. Each contractor hired their own personnel, making a total of eighty-five people working in cubicles in one large room. It became apparent to me and my partner that the only way to become a successful team was to make rules for how we would treat each other. It was the first order of business. They were:

- Attack the process, never the person.

- If we take good care of each other, the job will take care of itself.

The next challenge was to produce an electronic flow chart which displayed all the steps in the process. Using that chart as our central tracking tool enabled us to keep everyone informed, helped clarify our constantly changing projections, and kept us on schedule.

Frustrations would come up. The chart would identify the problem and who was responsible for it. We then worked together to come up with solutions. That was the secret: the commitment to one another's success.

To help manage the stress, I came up with ideas about supporting good working relationships. We developed a sense of family in our office. It included "family fun factors," such as monthly potlucks in the office conference room, learning how to line-dance in the parking lot after work, brown bag lunches during which each contractor taught us what it took to do their part of the job, and we rang a bell on the wall whenever anyone achieved one of their goals. Everyone stood up and cheered. When we needed a smile, I might put on my red clown nose.

I listened and coached when issues needed to be resolved. As an example, Linda came into my office early one morning weeping. It was the day her contract with us was ending. She told me her husband had surprised her by asking for a divorce during breakfast. She was devastated. I wanted to help. I asked her, "What's something you've always wanted to do with your life?"

"I'd love to live in San Francisco," she said, her eyes beginning to dry.

"Looks like the Universe is giving you a chance to begin your life over," I said. "It's like a blank canvas. Think of what your dream life would look like. Use those ideas to paint that picture." She sat up straighter in her chair, looking a little excited, and we explored possibilities for her. When we were finished Margaret left with hope in her eyes.

Linda's happiness mattered to me and my fellow workers knew I felt that way about each of them. We were family. We finished our project together on time and under budget!

🗝 **Honoring the process, working hard while caring for one another and having fun can accomplish the impossible.**

THREE SURVIVAL TECHNIQUES
1995

B eing the boss was far more demanding than I thought it would be when I took the job. It was inspiring to be in the right place at the right time doing what I instinctively knew to do. Each day figuring out how the team could solve the next problem and keep everyone feeling cared for and appreciated was complex and fun. I walked around the office each morning checking people's stress level, reminding them to take a deep breath. And sometimes I brought fresh cinnamon rolls from an old fashioned bakery near my house, which worked wonders.

There were often people waiting in line outside the small window-lit office our lead engineer and I shared. Phones rang and many e-mails awaited a response. There was meeting after meeting. My assistant did her best to help me, but many of the questions needed to be addressed by me.

After waiting her turn, Kathy came into our office. She was in charge of planning and zoning approvals, which were required to build our towers. She performed her duties in a professional and efficient manner. She had a quick and funny sense of humor while supervising her staff of eight. Later we became good friends. That day she sat down across from my desk while I was checking a couple of e-mails. I looked up and she quietly asked, "How do you work in this chaos? I never see you get upset or angry."

At that point I pulled my red nose from my pocket, put it on, sat back, and without much thought responded, "I think this helps, don't you?" Kathy burst out laughing.

Then I took my nose off and said, "Well, to really answer your question, three thoughts just came to mind. Here's what I try to do: Pay attention (the hardest one), take good care of myself, and focus on just what is in front of me." Then I explained how I practice them.

Pay attention means remember to take a deep breath, notice people's body language, listen with my heart as well as my head, and assess the energy around me and those I work with.

Take good care of myself means have something beautiful nearby to look at, do some yoga stretches, have a drink of water, go for a walking meeting outside, sit back in my chair, eyes closed, take some deep breaths and have healthy snacks handy. I always have lunch.

Work on just what is in front of me means keep the focus on one thing at a time and do it as well as I can before moving on to the next thing. I took a deep breath and added, "That's all I've got for that question. Does that help?"

Kathy smiled and said, "Very much, yes."

We finished the rest of our time with the business questions she'd brought. When she got up to leave I thought of one last thing and said, "Oh, you can borrow my red nose any time it gets too crazy! Or they're only a buck fifty at the costume shop nearby."

When we pay attention, care for ourselves and stay focused with humor, we may be more open-hearted, aware, and effective.

WHEN COMMUNICATION BREAKS DOWN

1996

It was an intense review meeting in our large window-lit conference room. Fifteen attendees represented all the managers of the six different groups working on our project. As the project manager, it was my job to discover why we were behind schedule. We needed to figure out the causes and solutions for the delays.

Chuck was the Construction Manager. He was a young, tall, slim, redheaded guy who was ambitious and not the best team player. Kim, on the other hand, was a quiet fellow; a professional and experienced lead engineer. When discussing the time it was taking engineering to choose a particularly difficult location, Chuck, looked across the table and said sarcastically, to Kim, "Well, we can't do our job if you don't do yours."

The unbreakable rule in our office was "attack the process and never the person". That rule had just been broken.

I put on the red nose which I always kept in my pocket. It was a tool I used to help manage the stress level in our office. It had a couple of uses. One was for making people smile and another was to interrupt an inappropriate conversation. What had just been said was inappropriate.

I stopped the meeting and said, "We are not proceeding until Kim tells Chuck how what was just said made him *feel*." Everyone at the table gasped. Kim started to defend the engineering position and I stopped him and said, "You are not telling Chuck how you *feel*." After a pause, Kim told Chuck, "What you just said was insulting and embarrassing." Chuck immediately apologized.

The meeting concluded successfully.

I asked Susan if she'd like to go to lunch. She was blonde, trim, and professional, wearing one of her suits from the sixties with some of her grandmother's matching green and gold jewelry. I admired her collectible wardrobe. We headed out to a nearby quiet little hole-in-the-wall restaurant serving sandwiches made with delicious homemade breads and organic veggies and meats.

On the way there, she said, "That was so shocking to have that kind of conversation in a business meeting!" Without thinking, I replied, "When communication breaks down, what's been lost is a safe place to tell the truth." That statement surprised both of us.

And laughingly she said, "Maybe you should write that down." And I did.

🗝 **A problem is best solved when put on the table, like a puzzle, so we can look at it as a process needing adjustment, rather than resorting to an attack making someone wrong.**

ARE YOU WILLING TO WORK WITH AN OPEN MIND?

1996

In my position as project manager, I had my hands full supervising the team of engineers, all male. I was female and not a technical person, though they liked my style of management. I was open to different strategies, was a good listener and mediator. And I made sure everyone was treated with respect.

Ed was one of my favorite engineers, but he had a stubborn streak. He was bright, and his ideas often had merit. Today we didn't agree.

He kept asking the same question over and over. I kept giving the answer I knew to be best for the project. It wasn't what he wanted to hear, so he ignored it. He had closed his mind.

I tried again. I gave him the answer on a piece of paper so he could see what I meant. He took the paper, looked at it, and frowned. He shook his head, as if I'd written it in Greek.

In an effort to tone things down, I leaned back in my chair, took a deep breath and waited for inspiration. Ed stood with his arms across his chest, a tower of righteousness so sure of himself—waiting for what I'd say next.

So I said to myself, "*He's made up his mind about how this should go and he's not going to accept any more information that he thinks may change his mind. It's over. No need to keep this little dance going. I'd trust him, but with a caveat.*"

Then I thought: "*We'll try it his way. It could be I've overlooked information he has, and he knows what he's talking about.*" I leaned forward, smiled and said. "Okay, let's try it your way. But there needs to be an approved backup plan if it doesn't work.

Do we have a deal?" He said, "Yes," then relaxed, and his frown disappeared as we shook hands.

I'd been like Ed myself in the past. I recognized in this spectacled young man an image of my own character at a younger age—at times fiercely holding on to my plans and seldom questioning my firm decisions.

Deeper listening and compromise may allow more flexible options.

SOMETIMES IT SEEMS JUST TOO MUCH

1996

I was in my office feeling completely over-whelmed. There were piles of paper on my desk and at my feet. The phone kept ringing. I had the answers, but was only one person, so some inquiries just had to go to voice mail. It felt like I wasn't making any headway.

At that moment, I took a deep breath, pushed my chair back and thought to my-self, "This chaos is only here for my enter-tainment. If I'm not having a good time, I can do something else." That made me smile.

My shoulders came down and I laid my head back on the chair. What a relief! Just then, my admin assistant, Joyce, came into my office with a deep frown on her young face.

I asked, "How's it going?"

"Not so well. I can't get the information I need from the construction group for our report due tomorrow because Jake is out sick. I haven't had time to reply to my e-mails and I'm behind updating the tracking system." She was totally stressed out, not at all like her. Joyce could handle anything—usually.

To lighten things up, I said to her, "You know, it seems to be a part of corporate culture to make us believe that if we don't make a deadline, someone will die. I've been here eleven years and haven't seen that happen yet. So, I will contact the manager of the construction group and see if I can get the info we need and you can take your lunch and get a breather."

Joyce laughed and looked relieved. It has been my philosophy for a long time that we often buy into the idea that being stressed, overly busy, and working too many hours is a sign of success and importance. The truth is, it's unhealthy.

At any moment we have the option to pause, feel renewed, and still be productive, even entertained!

STANDING TALL

1997

I knew there was tension in our office before I left for vacation, but I went anyway, hoping to return to a calm, cheerful atmosphere—but deep down I knew better. The trouble was too pervasive to disappear on its own.

One day, while I was resting and enjoying the beach in Oregon, the phone rang. Two loyal employees of mine called to tell me human resources had depicted me as "the victim of a textbook case of age/gender discrimination that should never happen again!" They were afraid for me. It was bad, and I knew it. I'd been documenting the situation for nine months, times when sexist comments were made or my authority was challenged or ignored by two subordinates who reported to me. The new management I reported to would not assist in rectifying the situation, either. "You should sue these guys," my employees said.

"You don't understand," I told them, "I don't know any good attorneys who would take on a case like this one. I don't have a snowball's chance in hell of winning."

"Have you got a pencil?" one of them asked. "Here's the name and number of one of the best attorneys in California. She specializes in employee law, and she's fabulous." I wrote down the info, thanked them and hung up.

I felt fearful, and my vacation was ruined. I knew that the office had moved to a new location while I was away. Prior to leaving, I had packed and sealed my boxes, but I dreaded seeing what had happened in my absence. Upon returning to the new location, I discovered I had been demoted from my position as operations manager to a lesser position without any title or job description.

What was supposed to be my new office had been converted into a conference room. I was assigned to a small cubicle and had no work to do. My original position was split into two, each taken over by a younger man. My carefully packed boxes had been opened. My day timer/calendar was missing as was my laptop computer. I was outraged!

I called that attorney. At my first visit, we talked for four hours, at no charge. I asked why she was interviewing me for so long and she said, "I'm figuring out how you would hold up under examination on the stand if we should go to trial. She continued, "Why would you put yourself through this?" I said, "It's not about money. What they did was wrong and I have enough evidence that they've been after me for months—just because I'm a successful middle-aged female manager. I want to sue them for the daughters and granddaughters who will come after me. If I don't hold those guys accountable for their wrong doing, then who will?" The attorney continued, "What are you most afraid of?"

I replied, "I'm frightened of being financially and professionally ruined."

After she had seen my extensive documentation, we proceeded to a lawsuit.

A year and a half later, I was emotionally spent, and the courts had begun moving toward decisions favoring employers rather than employees. We calculated the risk of trial and decided to negotiate a settlement which the opposition had already initiated.

When the case was settled, my attorney wrote me a letter affirming the wisdom of my decision to sue, stating, "You were an example and role model for others. You always maintained your integrity, and you made a positive difference in the way the women at the company are now treated. You impacted the men involved in the case for the "remainder of their lives." Plus, on the record, your managers had to admit that you were a very valued person in the company."

⚷ Living with integrity may require risking everything.

COMMUNICATION
IS THE KEY
1998

Jeri and Jim, Larry and Becky were two couples who had known each other for many years in their small hometown. Larry and Becky were retired and Jeri and Jim were homebuilders. They were considering putting together a partnership to begin a new business. They asked me if I would lead a strategic planning session with the four of them to see if this would be a good business decision. We met in a large room in a nearby office building.

After making some coffee, we sat down at a long conference table and got started.

It was time for me to ask concrete business questions and see if everyone was on the same page. We did it in a brainstorming format. Each person had a sticky note pad. They were to write down their answers on separate notes, and then we would put them together in categories on the white board on the wall.

The first question I asked was, "What are your personal expectations in this new business?" I asked them to write quickly to get their first thoughts. Each person finished their notes and Jim was done first. When I picked up Jim's only note, I saw exactly what I had expected from him. Jim was a master carpenter and an introvert. His note said, "I don't know."

I looked him in the eye and said, "Jim, 'I don't know' is not helpful. Each of you will be a viable partner in this business and bring many skills to the party. It is important that each of you understands what your partners' expectations are. If you don't know your expectations, you can't meet them.

Jim looked uncomfortable and was silent. I needed to explain my thinking to this practical, soft-spoken man with his slight build, brown eyes and thinning brown hair. I went on, trying not to show my exasperation. "You must have some idea of what you would like to have this business provide you. Your partners need to know that. If you were expecting something that was way outside the box, it might tell them this partnership is not viable." Jim looked skeptical, so I continued. "On the other hand, you may have expectations that resonate with and excite your partners. Saying 'I don't know' may be telling your partners you are withholding your wants and wishes. They could guess or assume what they are, try to achieve them, and miss the mark. Thus, everyone loses. I took a breath and waited. "What do you think, Jim?"

After pondering his answer, he sipped his coffee and agreed, filling out more information on his sticky notes. We resumed a very successful meeting.

A year later their business and partnership had become successful.

"I don't know at this moment, but I will get back to you with an answer" shows commitment to working with people.

PERMISSION
TO FAIL
2000

I had just arrived at the office in Arizona on Monday morning. Linda met me right at the door and said that Dani was crying. They didn't know why, but they wanted me to talk with her. I was worried and hoped that the matter was not too serious. Dani was a good worker and rarely got upset.

When I went into her office I found her sobbing. Her blonde hair was disheveled and she had mascara running down her cheeks. She didn't look like she'd gotten any sleep. I asked, "What's wrong, Dani?"

She said, "I have to pass the real estate test to get my real estate license or I won't get the promotion I desperately need! She blew her nose before saying more. "I studied on my own and a friend of mine, Lisa, who is a licensed realtor, helped me study in the evenings. I thought I was pretty well prepared when I went in to take the test Saturday. And I failed it!" she cried into a wet Kleenex and put her head down on the desk. She was sure she wouldn't be able to pass the test if she took it again.

I sat down next to her, held her hand and asked her to take a few deep breaths, one of my favorite cures for hysteria. Then I went and got her a drink of water. When I returned, Dani was a little calmer and I began to ask some questions.

"How many times can you take the test?"

"As many as I want."

"Does it matter how many times you fail?"

"No, it doesn't."

"Would your realtor friend still help you study some more?"

"Yes, I think so," she said sniffling.

"I have an idea. How about if you decided you'll fail the next test, but will pass it the third time? Think of it as a two-step process." I said.

Dani wiped her eyes and brightened up. She said she would try that and take the test on the following Saturday.

On Monday, she nearly tackled me as I came into the office. "I passed! I passed!" she yelled as she grabbed me.

"But, you weren't supposed to pass until the next test," I said. We hugged and laughed. All was well.

When the fear of failing is removed, it's possible to relax and be focused enough to succeed.

TIME TO QUIT

2001

The project in Riverside was not going well. The objectives kept changing, making progress difficult. The client's new person in charge didn't seem to understand his job, so he did not give us clear direction. My hands felt tied because of his incompetence. When they had called me in as a contractor to fix the problem, we were faced with the client's impossible timelines and confusion.

My team and I worked long hours, but with the continuous changes, the situation didn't improve. So the company hired two young attorneys to manage us. They decided we weren't working hard enough.

They wanted us to be in the office for 6:00am meetings every day! Some people had to drive in crazy California traffic for over an hour just to get to work.

I smelled a setup. The attorneys were planning for our team to fail so they could bring in their own team, get the billing for themselves, and push us out. I felt helpless to protect those who worked with me. It made me furious.

When I got to my apartment my frustrations came to a head. I realized I wasn't going to be able to pull the rabbit out of the hat—the attorneys were going to see to that. Then the phone rang. When she heard my voice, my daughter, Alicia, said, "You sound terrible!" And she listened as I unloaded my misery. I told her it was obvious that I needed to get out of that job.

"I have no idea where to go next or what to do!" I cried.

"Mom, remember how you taught us to always look at the worst thing that could happen when we had to make a decision?"

"Yes, I remember."

"Don't you get it? The worst thing that could happen to you is Paul!"

At first I didn't know what she meant. Then Alicia explained that if the job fell apart, I'd always have a place at their house—where I'd be with my son-in-law, Paul, whom I loved. He was my worst case scenario! I laughed through my tears. Bless my daughter for saving my sanity.

When I got off the phone, I loaded my belongings into boxes in preparation for leaving the very next morning. I was up at 5:30 am, packing everything into my rental car. Then I went into the office, handed in my resignation, and headed for the airport, and Arizona.

I left that job feeling such freedom and joy, knowing I'd land in a loving and safe place, no matter what.

In difficult times, trust the comfort and wisdom of those who love us.

IT'S WHAT WE ADMIRE IN OTHERS

1995

I had just arrived at my new office in California for the first time. I saw Mary as I walked in the door. She was an attractive professional-looking woman with medium length curly brown hair. Her lively blue eyes were set off by the navy jacket and skirt accented with silver jewelry. She came toward me smiling and introduced herself with a warm, firm handshake. Mary's demeanor made me feel welcome, and it was exciting to meet everyone.

A year later, my now dear friend, Mary said "When I first met you, you were so warm and open. I knew we would be instant friends."

She had become the best manager I had and made working on our project productive and fun. When the job was completed and she was leaving, she gave me high praise as a caring manager and leader. I thought about what she said and felt grateful for her appreciation.

I thanked her and looked at her smiling face. It came to me that I wanted her to know what I believed. I said, "We cannot recognize anything in another person that we do not already have in ourselves. Remember you have all the gifts you admire in me and can carry what you have learned with you to the next successful path of your own career. You have the "torch" now."

That's how we pass the "light" from one to another.

DENELLE "DENI" HARRIS lives in Prescott, Arizona, has education and training in counseling and is a certified Life Coach. Her stories come  out of her life experiences, including twenty seven years in a management capacity in corporate businesses including telecommunication. She is certified in the field of gerontology and has experience with remodeling and running a bed and breakfast.

She is currently on the board of directors of Girls Becoming Women, an organization mentoring young girls. Denelle teaches the popular Wise Women Gathering class at Yavapai Community College and shared her expertise with the Osher Lifelong Learning Institute (OLLI) for nine years.

May reading these stories awaken the treasure within you of your own stories.

68699329R00155

Made in the USA
Columbia, SC
11 August 2019